Dedication

I dedicate this book to our amazing children, Captain William Marshall Francis and Susan Marjorie Godfrey. From them, my wife, Marilyn, and I have learned valuable leadership principles and parenting skills. As dearly loved and highly respected adults, Billy and Susan model servant leadership in their personal lives and through their ministry and work. With the Apostle John, I affirm, "I have no greater joy than to hear that my children are walking in the truth" (3 John 1:4).

Building
Blocks
of Spiritual
Leadership

William W. Francis

TRIUMPH
PUBLISHING

CREST
BOOKS

Co-published by Crest Books and Triumph Publishing

Crest Books
The Salvation Army National Headquarters
615 Slaters Lane
Alexandria, VA 22313
Phone: 703/684-5523

Lt. Col. Allen Satterlee, Editor-in-Chief and National Literary Secretary
Roger Selvage, Art Director
Ashley Schena, Graphic Designer
Erin Thibeau, Editorial Assistant

Triumph Publishing
The Salvation Army Territorial Headquarters, Canada and Bermuda
2 Overlea Blvd
Toronto, ON M4H 1P4
Phone: 416/425-2111

Geoff Moulton, Editor-in-Chief and Literary Secretary

Available in print at www.salvationarmy.christianbook.com and as an
e-book at http://store.salvationarmy.ca or Amazon.com

ISBN: 978-0-9913439-5-9

Library of Congress Control Number: 2014944490

Printed in the United States of America

Praise for
Building Blocks of
Spiritual Leadership

"Whenever William Francis puts pen to paper, it is eminently worth reading. No more so than when he is writing about spiritual leadership. This book is a wonderfully comprehensive coverage of the whole subject, giving clarity to leadership roles from many angles, both from biblical principles and practice and from his own experience. He wisely includes a very helpful section on advice to leaders. This is a book not to be missed by all who work within the wide range of spiritual leadership."

— General Eva Burrows, Retired International Leader, The Salvation Army

"Most everyone in the church today acknowledges a current crisis in leadership. Nothing speaks with greater authority to the current leadership malaise than the voice of an authentic spiritual leader. In *Building Blocks of Spiritual Leadership*, William Francis speaks with candor, humor and authenticity about the challenges and opportunities of this critical calling. Spiritual leaders will recognize themselves and find help to both understand and embrace their role. Leaders who are perplexed and frustrated will find sage advice in Francis' accumulated wisdom. This book will help those who stand on the threshold of a leadership role to construct a solid foundation for joyful service. *Building Blocks* is biblical, practical and accessible. Those who read this book will laugh and learn, engage and practice, grow and celebrate."

— Dr. Paul W. Chilcote, Academic Dean, Ashland Theological Seminary

"I recommend this thoughtful book to all in or preparing for Christian leadership. Bill Francis gives us an accessible, uncomplicated and refreshingly unpretentious volume. Appealing equally to mind and heart, it is eminently suitable for both personal reflection and group discussion."

— General Shaw Clifton, Retired International Leader, The Salvation Army

"In *Building Blocks of Spiritual Leadership,* William Francis takes a unique approach to understanding the requirements of spiritual leadership. The author presents 23 dimensions of leadership, weaving biblical and contemporary references into his analysis of each of them. The author's own experience as a leader underpins his later advice, both personal and substantive, for leaders."

— Gail Cook-Bennett, Chair of the Board of the Institute of Corporate Directors, Member of The Salvation Army's National Advisory Board (Canada and Bermuda)

"Spiritual leadership is about character, conviction and above all Christlikeness. We must therefore be devoted followers of Jesus before we seek to lead others in his name. As Jesus sacrificed his life for the redemption of creation, so the offering of our lives as his coworkers must be characterized by a divinely inspired zeal to accompany, lift up, help, support and nurture God's people. Such a leadership model is radical, countercultural, transformative and ably articulated by Commissioner Francis, whose book I am most pleased to endorse."

— General André Cox, International Leader, The Salvation Army

"This book is a winner not only because William Francis covers a remarkable number of leadership skills, but also because he speaks out of a long and fruitful life of dedicated leadership. Commissioner Francis addresses integrity, productivity, attitude, humor and more. A must read for wannabe leaders and, in fact, all leaders."

— Dr. Donald E. Demaray, Senior Beeson Professor of Preaching (R), Asbury Theological Seminary

"This book is written by someone who knows what spiritual leadership is all about. Commissioner Bill Francis served in various leadership capacities during his long and distinguished vocation as a Salvation Army officer. The book begins with a critical reminder—that spiritual leadership derives its authority from the Scriptures, and the biblical leader is rooted in Christ. And then the author takes the reader right into servant leadership, the hallmark of the Christian leader. The remaining chapters flow from this significant insight and are grounded in Scripture. All who read this book will be both nurtured and inspired as they seek to be the kind of leader pleasing to our Lord."

— *Dr. Roger J. Green, Professor and Chair of Biblical Studies and Christian Ministries, Gordon College*

"This book answers the age-old question: is a leader born or made? The answer to both is yes: spiritual leaders are born again and made. This book comes from years of context. There are tons of great encouragements and challenges in this book. This is a must-read for anyone seeking to grow as a follower of Jesus. Leadership is influence, and anyone who is growing in their faith should find themselves increasing in their influence."

— *Commissioner David E. Jeffrey, National Commander, The Salvation Army*

"Just when you thought you had read enough about leadership, Commissioner Bill Francis produces this excellent work. Having benefited from his spiritual leadership in my journey and knowing his advanced intellect, I was immediately drawn into this timely and appropriate work. Defining the aspects of leadership and giving advice for all leaders, the Commissioner generously shares with us this applicable guide for this generation. You will be a better leader for reading it."

— *Commissioner James M. Knaggs, The Salvation Army*

"Leadership is about influence … the first person you must influence is you, with the very best habits possible. A great leader serves his/her staff and very often demonstrates quiet sacrifice for the betterment of the organization. Commissioner Francis' new book delivers on all fronts with powerful, biblical truths that you should not waver from. Buy and read this book and put these principles into your life and business and you will be an influencer."

— *Dr. Peter Legge, Chairman and CEO, Canada Wide Media Limited*

"In today's world, leaders need to be more than just skilled professionals with a vision; they must also provide their organizations with a strong moral compass. In *Building Blocks of Spiritual Leadership,* William Francis tackles leadership challenges with unflinching honesty and gives readers a powerful lesson in how to develop their own leadership style. Wonderfully researched and insightful, this book offers concrete, actionable advice on current best practices in leadership, many of which are rooted in Christianity."

— Andrew Lennox, Senior Vice President, Scotiabank,
Chair of The Salvation Army's National Advisory Board (Canada and Bermuda)

"Commissioner Francis has drawn from his vast experience and deep reflection to put manageable pieces of the complex leadership puzzle into your hands. His heart for your effectiveness, coupled with his passion for God, make this a practical and stimulating read. It's as if you get a chance to sit one on one with him and glean insight that will immediately translate into your own life."

— Dr. Kevin W. Mannoia, Chaplain and Professor, Azusa Pacific University,
Chairman of the Wesleyan Holiness Consortium

"*Building Blocks of Spiritual Leadership* does something most leadership books do not. It respects the fact that busy leaders don't have time to read long theories or complex models; it gets straight to the point. Filled with practical insights, this is a book that instructs and inspires. We need to be spiritually fed and encouraged, and we need to find a way forward for ourselves and those we lead. If you do not see yourself in this book, perhaps you will see the leader you can become."

— Commissioner Susan McMillan, Territorial Commander,
Canada and Bermuda Territory, The Salvation Army

"Commissioner Francis consistently targets the essence and form of leadership and provides reliable signposts which, when followed, can inhibit personal derailment and chart a positive course for every leader. The book is perceptive and practical and a good read, 'for such a time as this,' for all leaders."

— Commissioner Brian Peddle, International Zonal Secretary
of the Americas and Caribbean, The Salvation Army

"This is a book to savor slowly. Commissioner Francis writes practically and provocatively, making judicious use of his wide reading in leadership literature. The book has special authority and resonance for me because I have served with the author and know him to be an exemplar of the principles and practices he commends."

— *Lt. Colonel Lyell M. Rader Jr., The Salvation Army*

"In *Building Blocks of Spiritual Leadership,* Commissioner William Francis gives the reader an abundance of wisdom from a lifetime of Spirit-led leadership in The Salvation Army at the national and international levels. His insights are nuanced by a long history of Christian college and university board governance as well. With biblically based insight refined in the crucible of experience, his writings give us a fresh look at what it means to lead in the Spirit."

— *Dr. Jonathan S. Raymond, President Emeritus and Senior Fellow, Trinity Western University*

"Christian leadership is a complex concept and an even more complex reality. Francis has the credentials to tackle the job of making it clearer. The result is a book filled with nuggets of wisdom, insightful readings of the Bible, and useable tactics. We need more leaders with the character and savvy this book advocates."

— *Dr. James E. Read, Executive Director, The Salvation Army Ethics Centre*

"Commissioner Francis succinctly and artfully captures the spiritually-inspired and pragmatic traits that are so clearly resident in the lives of Salvationist leaders whom I have admired over the years. Leaders of every calling will be challenged by reflecting on these principles."

— *Steve Reinemund, Former Dean of Wake Forest School of Business, Retired Chairman and CEO of PepsiCo*

"*Building Blocks of Spiritual Leadership* provides the leader of today with the perfect reference guide as we aspire to lead as God has called us to in the roles he has placed us. The Scripture backing up each leadership trait in each chapter supplies the reader with a rich foundation. The challenge of leadership as described can inspire each one of us to press on and try to make a positive difference in the lives of people. I urge you to read this book and use its building blocks as you lead."

— Diane Paddison, Founder of 4word, Member of The Salvation Army's
National Advisory Board

"In this work, Commissioner Francis delineates Christian leadership principles and illustrates the same from Scripture, Church history and contemporary life. *Building Blocks of Spiritual Leadership* is comprised of 33 concise, insightful chapters, covering a wide range of topics, which not only define the nature of spiritual leadership, but also offer helpful advice on how to effectively lead as followers of Christ."

— Dr. R. David Rightmire, Professor of Bible and Theology, Asbury University

"In a vivid, insightful, inspiring and broad-gauged way, William Francis explores amazing variations of spiritual leadership. He draws on a wide range of sources, particularly biblical concepts of Christian leadership rooted in a continuous trustful relationship. He emphasizes the leader's acceptance of a compelling personal call by God. Francis reflects a wide variety of wise non-Christian authors as well as Christian writers, not even omitting science fiction and stories of comic strips. The guideposts Francis provides will help leaders reflect upon their call and the way they act in relation to others. These are all put into a helpful order, giving rules and shortcuts to easily recollect. The book is written in a pleasant balance of open-mindedness while deeply rooted in Scripture and passionately focused on mission. Francis avoids using typical Christian insider language without sacrificing profound, important and precise communication. This book revived me from the first to the last line. I found myself laughing out loud at the profound humor. This book is both stimulating and really needed!"

— Dr. Ulrike Schuler, Professor of Church History,
Methodism and Ecumenism, Reutlingen School of Theology

Contents

PART I: THE LEADER

PART II: ADVICE FOR LEADERS

Foreword

I t takes a leader to make things happen. When God wanted the Israelites to leave Egypt he did not appoint an escape committee, he appointed a leader. When major international businesses are in trouble they do not appoint a new board, they headhunt throughout the world until they find the man or woman who will lead them to success.

William Booth felt so strongly about the leadership principle that when he created The Salvation Army he wrote into its constitution that the Army must forever be "under the oversight, direction and control of some one person."

It takes a leader to make things happen in the local church or Salvation Army corps. It is no secret that having an inspirational leader at the apex of the church pyramid makes all the difference. But a local church needs far more than just one leader; it needs many. For within each church a range of groups and fellowships are at work, and having an inspirational leader at the apex of each of these pyramids is equally vital. Therefore, not just few but many within the church are called to be leaders. And with spiritual leadership being uniquely demanding and many-sided, they need all the support they can be given. In this book, William Francis provides them with a barrowful of blocks for the building up of inspirational spiritual leadership that will make things happen. These building blocks are designed for all who, by calling or appointment, stand at the apex of a pyramid—whether large or small, high or low—within the Christian church. No leader exists who does not need them, for, as the author writes, "spiritual leaders are both 'born' and 'made' ... and effective spiritual leadership results from a dynamic combination of gift and grit, skill and sweat, innate ability and intense work."

As an exceptional Army leader and teacher, William Francis makes the building blocks clear and concise, pithy and practical. Even the table of contents is a joy to read, revealing the multitude of spiritual leadership aspects touched on in the book. Mixing the wisdom of Scripture with the insights of secular and spiritual leaders past and present, and sprinkling the pages with anecdotes and quotes, the author brings his points to life and makes them memorable. No building block is so heavy that it cannot be lifted.

This is a book to read through and return to, point by point, for meditation, personal application and prayer. Leaders serving in the church today and those who in the future will set out on the path of leadership owe much to the author, and on their behalf I say thank you to Commissioner William Francis.

— *John Larsson, General (Retired)*
The Salvation Army

Preface

You may be thinking: "Not another leadership book!" Indeed, if you search "leadership" on Amazon.com, you will find over 300,000 results. Few terms have more matches. Who has not been drawn to a leadership book that promises to transform our leadership and our lives? Therefore, I understand asking, "So what? Why another book on leadership?" I am well acquainted with the question. I have been trained to ask "So what?" before submitting the final draft of a presentation, article or book to be considered for publication. My loved and respected mentor, Colonel Henry Gariepy, now departed, instilled in me the habit of asking this tough question once completing a final draft. "Put the paper down," Hank counseled, "and ask out loud the question, 'So what?'" He went on to instruct, "If the 'so what' question cannot be adequately answered, tear up the manuscript and start over!" The fact that you are now reading these words shows that I have been able to answer the dreaded question to my satisfaction.

Throughout my life I have looked for simple, succinct ways to remember important, complicated facts. Hence, I find myself quietly singing a Sunday school refrain to find a Bible passage: "Genesis, Exodus, Leviticus, Numbers, Deuteronomy …" I convert Celsius to Fahrenheit by doubling the Celsius figure, adding 30 and subtracting from the total one degree for every 5 degrees, starting with 15 of the original Celsius number. My family and friends insist that this is not the simple way to convert, but it works for me.

In this book I attempt to distill the basic building blocks of leadership in general, and the essential elements of servant leadership as described and mandated in the Bible specifically. By no means is this book exhaustive, nor have I attained mastery over any of the aspects of leadership. To the contrary, I have much more to learn, and much more to become, on the journey to being a consistent spiritual leader. My prayer is that this concise volume will serve as a basis for the reader's continued study and modeling of biblically centered spiritual leadership.

The seeds of this book began in the summer of 1996. While enrolled in a doctoral program at Fuller Theological Seminary, I took a course on servant leadership from Dr. Patrick (Pat) Lattore and Dr. Robert (Bob) S. Paul. Our cohort met in Aspen, Colorado for two weeks—a fortnight that radically changed my understanding of leadership. In addition to the full days of academic classes, discussion groups, personal study and a group analysis of the newly released film "First Knight," we participated in an adventurous one-day learning experience of white water rafting down the Arkansas River, where our esteemed professor Pat fell overboard. We had the overwhelming satisfaction of rescuing him. I owe much to the course leaders, Pat and Bob. I learned more about leadership as a result of this course than through any other single academic or practical endeavor. It caused a profound paradigm shift in my understanding of the requisites for ministry and the role of a servant leader.

I have written this book in the spirit of finding simple ways to remember essential leadership principles. I trust the reader will find reading it far easier than memorizing temperature conversion computations.

— *William W. Francis*

Acknowledgements

I am truly grateful to those who inspired me to write this book and to everyone who extended encouragement, assistance and prayer support. I am especially indebted to the following family members and friends:

My devoted, Spirit-filled wife of nearly 50 years, Marilyn, and our beloved children, Billy and Susan, as well as their cherished spouses, Annalise and Robert, for their enduring inspiration, affirming encouragement and abiding patience.

My literary mentors over the past half-century, including Dr. Donald Demaray, Lt. Colonel William MacLean, Colonel Henry Gariepy, Lt. Colonel Marlene Chase, and Linda Johnson, who have had a profound influence on my writing. I thank the Lord for bringing these esteemed colleagues and dear friends into my life.

Major Peter Farthing, who, as editor of *The Officer* magazine, first asked me to write a series on the essentials of spiritual leadership. Peter is not only a respected colleague and literary guide, he became and remains a valued, caring and supportive friend, as are the editors who followed, Majors Ed Forster and Charles King. The series in *The Officer* lasted from 1999 to 2006 and spanned portions of the international leadership of Generals Paul Rader, John Gowans and John Larsson, who each actively supported the series.

Lt. Colonel Jim Champ, Communications Secretary for the Canada and Bermuda Territory (Toronto, Ontario), and his successor Geoff Moulton, Editor-in-Chief and Literary Secretary, who both advocated expanding *The Officer* series into a book. In addition, the Territorial Literature Council unreservedly gave their invaluable support for the project.

Major Fred Ash, who painstakingly arranged the series into chapters, skillfully edited the individual articles and helped mold them into a unified book.

Brandon Laird, for his skillful design of the e-book being published by Triumph Publishing, as well as the publications department of the Canada and Bermuda Territory.

Lt. Colonel Allen Satterlee, Editor-in-Chief and National Literary Secretary for USA National Headquarters (Alexandria, Virginia), who collaborated with his Canadian counterpart, Geoff Moulton, in this historic joint publishing venture, the first between Crest Books and Triumph Publishing.

Judith Brown, Editorial Assistant at USA National Headquarters, whose vital expertise and personal commitment to the project is sincerely appreciated, and Erin Thibeau, her successor. I am grateful to Erin for her professionalism and expertise through the final stages of publication.

Roger Selvage, for his exceptional work creating the design for the Crest Book edition, and the rest of the publications staff at USA National Headquarters.

My respected colleagues, for their insightful scrutiny of the manuscript and generous endorsements: General Eva Burrows, Dr. Paul Chilcote, General Shaw Clifton, Gail Cook-Bennett, General André Cox, Dr. Donald Demaray, Dr. Roger Green, Commissioner David Jeffrey, Commissioner James Knaggs, Peter Legg, Andrew Lennox, Dr. Kevin Mannoia, Commissioner Susan McMillan, Diane Paddison, Commissioner Brian Peddle, Lt. Colonel Dr. Lyell Rader, Dr. Jonathan Raymond, Dr. James Read, Steve Reinemund, Dr. David Rightmire and Dr. Ulrike Schuler.

General John Larsson, now retired, who personified servant leadership during his tenure as The Salvation Army's International Leader (2002-2006), in which *The Officer* ran nearly half of the original series. I deeply appreciate his willingness to provide the book's foreword.

Above all, I acknowledge the abiding love and grace of the Lord, who through the Holy Spirit, has promised to "guide [us] into all truth" (John 16:13).

Chapter 1: *Motivated Leader*

Books and audio recordings on leadership cram bookstore shelves. I have read and heard them all, or so it seems. In truth, my personal study, though well stocked, probably includes less than five percent of what is on the market. More often than not, the material is insightful and helpful. Most leadership resources have their source and focus in the corporate world, but their concepts are often transferable to Christian ministry.

However, every book or audio recording created from a secular perspective reveals that spiritual leadership is fundamentally different from that of business or politics. Indeed, in many ways, they are diametrically opposed. Henri Nouwen sagely observed:

> **Christian leaders cannot simply be persons who have well-informed opinions about the burning issues of our time. Their leadership must be rooted in the permanent, intimate relationship with the incarnate Word, Jesus, and they need to find there the source for their words, advice, and guidance ... Dealing with burning issues without being rooted in a deep personal relationship with God easily leads to divisiveness because, before we know it, our sense of self is caught up in our opinion about a given subject. But when we are securely rooted in personal intimacy with the source of life, it will be possible to remain flexible without being relativistic, convinced without being rigid, willing to confront without being offensive, gentle and forgiving without being soft, and true witnesses without being manipulative.[1]**

Nouwen calls every Christian leader to embody what he characterizes as Christian leadership.

The Bible teaches that the desire to become a leader is a commendable goal. The apostle Paul reminded his young protégé Timothy that, "to aspire to leadership is an honorable ambition" (1 Timothy 3:1, NEB). However, conditions in Paul's day were very different. Leadership positions such as bishop or overseer were not coveted in the first-century Church. Early Church leaders faced life-threatening dangers and carried grave responsibilities. In times of persecution, the leader drew the fire. The leader was the first to suffer and the first to die. Therefore, few sought office for selfish reasons; it was too dangerous. The apostle was providing incentive and praise for those who were willing to take the risk.

In most of the world today, Christian leadership accords prestige and privilege, not pain and penalty. There remain, of course, parts of the world where church leaders are severely persecuted, and Paul's words to them ring ever true. Yet in large measure, Christian leadership today carries great inducement for self-seeking, unspiritual men and women to hold some prestigious office or rank.

As spiritual leaders, we must heed Jeremiah's warning to Baruch. Jeremiah counseled, "Should you then seek great things for yourself? Seek them not" (Jeremiah 45:5). Jeremiah's caution to Baruch must be held in constant tension with Paul's admonition to Timothy. Christians can and should aspire to leadership, but their motivation must be selfless. Herein lies the paradox of spiritual leadership.

Again, Nouwen expresses it well: "I leave you with the image of the leader with outstretched hands, who chooses a life of downward mobility. It is the image of the praying leader, the vulnerable leader, the trusting leader. May that image fill our hearts with hope, courage, and confidence."[2]

Chapter 2: *Servant Leader*

God alone calls, equips and sustains His spiritual leaders. The Bible proclaims, "No one from the east or the west or from the desert can exalt a man. But it is God who judges: He brings one down, he exalts another" (Psalm 75:6-7). Throughout Scripture, we encounter God searching for a particular person for a specific task: "The Lord has sought out a man after His own heart" (1 Samuel 13:14). "Go up and down the streets of Jerusalem, look around and consider ... if you can find but one person who deals honestly and seeks the truth" (Jeremiah 5:1). "I looked for a man among them who would ... stand before Me in the gap" (Ezekiel 22:30).

In understanding the biblical concepts of a spiritual leader and servant leadership, the words "leader" and "leadership" require careful definition. These words are of modern origin and are largely unique to the English language. "Leadership" words developed parallel to the decline of monarchies and the rise of democracies in the twentieth-century.

Leadership language has dramatically increased in modern translations of the Bible. The King James Version (1611) uses "leader" only three times as a translation for the original Hebrew words (1 Chronicles 12:27, 13:1; Isaiah 55:4). Twentieth-century translations progressively increase the usage of leadership language to more accurately translate the Hebrew, Greek and Aramaic originals. The Revised Standard Version (1946-52) expands the use of "leader" and "leadership" to 52 times; the New American Standard Bible (1959-71), 65 times; the New International Version (1973-74), 81 times; and the New Revised Standard Version (1989) uses "leader" and its derivatives a record 110 times.

We need to be careful to adopt a truly biblical understanding of this relatively modern concept. In his doctoral dissertation, *Theology, Theory*

& Practice of Leadership (Fuller Theological Seminary), Dr. Robert S. Paul notes: "If we can hear God clearly on what it means to be a leader, then many other things fall into place … As practicing leaders, we traffic constantly in things that are particularly prone to idolatrous distortion: the nature of power, the source of human meaning, the definition of achievement, and the value of the other person."

The New Testament teaches that leaders must primarily be servants. The Greek word that best describes the essence of spiritual leadership is *doulos*, meaning a bondservant, a slave. *Doulos* defines a Christian's relationship to Christ. It is invariably used in contrast to the description of Jesus as *kurios*, meaning lord and master. Jesus is Lord. As Christian leaders, we are not masters but slaves of the Master.

Several of Paul's epistles begin with the reminder that the writer is a slave (*doulos*) and Jesus is master and lord (*kurios*). For example, the book of Romans begins, "Paul a servant of Jesus Christ, called to be an apostle and set apart for the gospel of God … regarding His son … who through the Spirit of holiness was declared with power to be the Son of God by His resurrection from the dead: Jesus Christ our Lord" (Romans 1:1-4). See also James 1:1, 2 Peter 1:1 and Jude 1. This kind of submission to Christ is at the heart of the servant leader.

Commissioner Samuel Logan Brengle, one of The Salvation Army's distinguished leaders, summarized the road to spiritual authority and leadership:

> **[Leadership] is not won by promotion, but by many prayers and tears. It is attained by confessions of sin, and much heart-searching and humbling before God; by self-surrender, a courageous sacrifice of every idol, a bold, deathless, uncompromising and uncomplaining embracing of the Cross, and by an eternal, unfaltering looking unto Jesus crucified. It is not gained by seeking great things for ourselves, but rather, like Paul, by counting those things that are gain to us a loss for Christ. That is a great price, but it must be unflinchingly paid by him who would be not merely a nominal but a real spiritual leader of men, a leader whose power is recognized and felt in heaven, on earth and in hell.[3]**

Spiritual leaders must continually pay the high price of their divine calling, considering "everything a loss compared to the surpassing greatness of knowing Christ Jesus my Lord" (Philippians 3:8).

Chapter 3: *Shepherd Leader*

Whether religious or secular, every organization possesses only one genuine resource—its membership. People are more valuable than the bottom line and more crucial than any other tangible resource.

Dr. Kenneth C. Haugk, Lutheran pastor and cofounder of Stephen Ministries, laments the belief that a pastor is the leader of ministry and the congregants are the spectators. This perspective, says Dr. Haugk, "has been a major stumbling block to the modern Church." Indeed, the Church that Jesus admonished, "feed my sheep," has repeatedly failed to engage its congregations in the essential task of increasing the flock. The Great Commission (Matthew 28:19-20) has become the great omission of the modern Church.

In biblical times, people understood the close relationship of a shepherd to his flock. The gospel narrative records that "when [Jesus] saw the crowds, He had compassion on them, because they were harassed and helpless, like sheep without a shepherd. Then He said to His disciples, 'The harvest is plentiful but the workers are few. Ask the Lord of the harvest, therefore, to send out workers into His harvest field'" (Matthew 9:36-38). The image of the shepherd with his sheep is woven into the language of the Bible. Even today, flocks of sheep blanket Judea's central plateau, which stretches 35 miles from Bethel to Hebron and varies from 14 to 17 miles in width. In biblical times, as now, the most familiar figure of the Judean uplands was the shepherd.

The shepherd's life was hard. He was never off duty, as no flock ever grazed without a shepherd. The sparse grass induced the sheep to wander. Without protective walls, the sheep required constant attention. On either side of the relatively slender Judean plateau the ground dipped sharply into the desert to the east and the coastal plain to the west. The shepherd's lonely task was constant and dangerous.

God entrusts spiritual leaders, whether lay or clergy, as shepherds of His people. The Greek word for shepherd, *poimaine*, reveals that the shepherd-leader is "one who feeds and nurtures the flock." Peter encourages Christian leaders to "be shepherds of God's flock that is under your care ... not because you must, but because you are willing, as God wants you to be; not greedy for money, but eager to serve; not lording over those entrusted to you, but being examples to the flock. And when the Chief Shepherd appears, you will receive the crown of glory that will never fade away" (1 Peter 5:2-4).

Biblical images of the shepherd illustrate the spiritual leader's responsibility to love, nurture and guide those under his or her care. The shepherd had absolute responsibility to protect and nurture his flock. He accomplished his task by first insuring that he maintained his own health. He employed all his tools and skills to feed, defend and guide his flock.

The hymn writer Charles Wesley captured in verse the essence of the shepherd's prayer, every spiritual leader's petition: "Help us to help each other, Lord / Each other's cross to bear; / Let each his friendly aid afford, / And feel his brother's care."

God alone chooses men and women for the extraordinary task of shepherding His people. Spiritual leaders are called, ordained and equipped for the sacred responsibility of caring for their God-given flock. The call to leadership is individual, and it is specific. "You did not choose me," Jesus reminds His disciples, "but I chose you and appointed you." He specifically calls His servant leaders to feed His sheep (John 15:16; John 21:15-17).

First-century shepherds carried four indispensable pieces of equipment. Each tool provides an analogue to twenty-first-century ministry. The first essential tool was the shepherd's scrip, a bag made of animal skin in which he carried food. The shepherd had to remain healthy and strong in order to aggressively protect the flock. The importance of taking care of one's self is a hard lesson for the spiritual leader to learn. Leaders must continually heed Paul's admonition: "Don't you know that you yourselves are God's temple and that God's Spirit lives in you? If anyone destroys God's temple, God will destroy him; for God's temple is sacred, and you are that temple" (1 Corinthians 3:16-17).

The remaining three tools were for feeding, nurturing and protecting the flock. Each shepherd treasured his custom-made sling. In the hands of a competent shepherd a sling became a lethal weapon. The Bible describes the skill of some of Israel's finest warriors as men who "could sling a stone at a hair and not miss" (Judges 20:16).

The shepherd's rod was a short wooden club that hung from his belt by a leather thong. The rod aided the shepherd in defending himself and his flock against beasts and robbers. Once a day, the rod doubled as a diagnostic instrument. When the sheep returned to the fold at the close of the day, the shepherd held the rod across the narrow entrance and close to the ground. As each sheep passed under the rod, the shepherd performed a quick examination to see if the sheep showed signs of disease or injury. Spiritual leaders take their example from God Himself, who declared, "I will take note of you as you pass under my rod, and I will bring you into the bond of the covenant" (Ezekiel 20:37).

The final piece of the shepherd's equipment was the staff, which has become symbolic of his vocation. With his staff he could catch and retrieve sheep that had strayed from the flock. He also used the staff to dig holes at the edge of a stream so the sheep could drink from the still water (sheep cannot drink flowing water). Finally, the staff provided a much needed walking cane for the long days of standing and walking.

The biblical image of the shepherd illustrates and defines the Christian leader's responsibility to love, nurture and guide those under his or her care. Spiritual leaders accomplish their tasks by first maintaining their own spiritual and physical health and then employing all their tools and skills to care for the flock. Trustworthy spiritual leaders must follow the Lord's example: "He tends His flock like a shepherd: He gathers the lambs in His arms and carries them close to His heart; He gently leads those that have young" (Isaiah 40:11).

Chapter 4: *Follower Leader*

inding Scripture passages that focus primarily on leadership is challenging. In his celebrated book, *A Church for the 21st Century*, Leith
Anderson observes:

> It should surprise us that so much is said [today] about leaders and so
> little about followers, especially among Christians committed to the
> Bible. The Bible says comparatively little about leadership and a great
> deal about followership. Jesus did not invite Peter, Andrew, James, and
> John to become leaders. He said, "Follow Me."⁴

From a biblical perspective, spiritual leadership is solely dependent
upon faithful discipleship. As with His first-century disciples, Jesus wants
His twenty-first-century servant leaders to be followers first. Douglas K.
Smith states the biblical axiom:

> In the twenty-first-century organization, all leaders must learn to
> follow if they are to successfully lead ... Leaders at all levels and in all
> situations must pay close attention to situations in which their most
> effective option is to follow—not because the hierarchy demands they
> "obey," but because performance requires them to rely on the capacities
> and insights of other people.⁵

Following is at the heart of being a spiritual leader. Jesus' disciples
learned to lead by following Him, literally and figuratively. As with most
first-century rabbis, Jesus was a peripatetic teacher—He taught as he
walked, and the disciples followed Him.

The image of disciples learning from Jesus "on the move" has had a
profound effect on my personal study habits and decision-making. I often

imagine myself walking and talking with the Master, and now and then I hear Him say, "Follow Me." I vicariously empathize with Thomas as he questions, "How can we know the way?" In the midst of the most difficult leadership decisions, I have wanted to say to Thomas, "I know what you mean. How can I know the right way forward?" Jesus' answer remains forever the same. He reminds us, "I am the way and the truth and the life" (John 14:5-6). Jesus, the Light of the World, promised, "Whoever follows Me will never walk in darkness, but will have the light of life" (John 8:12). As human beings, we are bound to stumble in the darkness when we walk alone. When we walk in the light, however, we will never falter.

The classical Greek word for "follow," *akoloutheo,* appears 89 times in 86 verses of the New Testament. This word is used exclusively to describe following Christ. The one exception is found in Mark 14:13, when Jesus instructs His disciples to "go into the city, and a man carrying a jar of water will meet you. Follow him." Even this exception is a command from Jesus.

Akoloutheo has five meanings. It is noteworthy that all five meanings describe fundamental aspects of the spiritual leader's relationship to the Master. When Jesus said, "Follow Me," I believe that he applied all five meanings. The follower of Christ, and especially the servant leader, must follow the Master as a soldier following his captain; as a slave accompanying his master; as a patient accepting a counselor's opinion; as a citizen obeying the laws of the land; and as a student following a teacher's line of argument.

Where will the journey of following Jesus end? At the cross! J. Oswald Sanders reminds leaders that "a cross stands in the way of spiritual leadership, a cross upon which the leader must be impaled. Heaven's demands are absolute: 'He laid down His life for us: and we ought to lay down our lives for the brethren' (1 John 3:16)."[6]

Jesus' call to follow Him and to shepherd His followers is a call to die with Him. Christ's call to His disciples, His spiritual leaders, reverberates over two millennia: "If anyone would come after Me, he must deny himself and take up his cross and follow Me. For whoever wants to save his life will lose it, but whoever loses his life for Me will find it" (Matthew 16:24-25). C. Gene Wilkes captures the essence of this spiritual reality:

Jesus was more interested in His disciples' willingness to follow Him to the cross than in their ambition to hold places of power in His kingdom. Ambition is not the same thing as willingness to follow Jesus to the cross. Jesus cared that His followers were willing to obey him."[7]

As with Peter, Jesus' first and last words of instruction remain the same for His spiritual leaders today: "Follow Me!" (Matthew 4:19; John 21:19).

Chapter 5: *Spirit-filled Leader*

Leadership is not essentially positional. While position and rank serve to define the parameters of responsibility, neither ensures competent leadership. Position only defines bestowed responsibility, not competency or effectiveness. Leadership is not singular, either. The leader and follower are vitally interrelated. The gifts, perceptions and needs of the follower are crucial to the success of the leader. Effective leaders understand, value and strive to meet the needs and expectations of their followers. It is the follower who verifies genuine leadership. The outcome of good leadership is to have a *community* of power, not a *position* of power. Leaders who look for their source of power in assigned position alone are doomed to personal and professional failure. Genuine spiritual leadership is larger than a position or a person.

The greatest leaders throughout history have been men and women lacking conferred positions. Renowned non-positional leaders include Mahatma Gandhi, Martin Luther King Jr., Mother Teresa and Nelson Mandela, to name a few. Gandhi, King and Mandela battled racial prejudice and injustice without the support of sanctioned platforms. Mother Teresa's caring, sacrificial ministry to India's poor resulted from her spiritual posture, not temporal position. Even Jesus lacked positional authority during his earthly life. He was an itinerant rabbi, lacking both political and ecclesiastical prestige and power. Competent, effective leaders such as these were not given positions of leadership initially; inward strength and character developed them into the leaders they were, and their power transcended their position.

"One of the outstanding ironies of history is the utter disregard of ranks and titles in the final judgments men pass on each other," remarked Com-

missioner Samuel Logan Brengle of The Salvation Army. "The final estimate
of men shows that history cares not an iota for the rank or title a man has
borne, or the office he has held, but only the quality of his deeds and the
character of his mind and heart."[8]

The end product of leadership must be community. Leadership has
everything to do with relationships and little to do with tasks. It is in the
life-changing relationships of love that we find true Christian leadership.
Jesus did not say, "If you feed My sheep, you love Me," He said, "If you
love Me, feed My sheep" (John 21:15-17).

When the burning zeal of first-century Christians resulted in the extraordinary growth of the apostolic Church, the disciples were forced to
recruit additional leaders. The everyday demands of the ministry resulted
in the need to appoint leaders to care for the neglected poor and widows.
The apostles clearly specified the type of person to be chosen: "Choose
seven men from among you who are known to be full of the Spirit and
wisdom. We will turn this responsibility over to them and will give our
attention to prayer and the ministry of the word" (Acts 6:3-5).

It is significant that the essential requirement for leadership in the
Church, even for what may be understood as secular service, was that
leaders were "full of the Spirit and wisdom." As J. Oswald Sanders notes,
leaders must be people of "*integrity*, of honest report; of *sagacity*, full of
wisdom; of *spirituality*, full of the Spirit. Spirituality is not easy to define
but its presence or absence can easily be discerned."[9]

If being filled with the Spirit is the basic requirement for those who
serve in the subordinate stations of Christian service, how much more is
required for those who are called to greater positions of responsibility?
Only Spirit-filled leaders who employ spiritual methods can accomplish
spiritual goals. What a far-reaching change would occur if we strictly
followed this leadership axiom. However brilliant, gifted or charming,
men and women who lack the power of the Holy Spirit have no place in
Church leadership.

Jesus summons spiritual leaders to a life and ministry of holiness. Being
filled with the Holy Spirit remains the indispensable requisite for leader-

ship. The divine imperative is as valid today as it was for His first-century leaders. Jesus commands us to "wait for the gift My Father promised, which you have heard Me speak about. For John baptized with water, but … you will be baptized with the Holy Spirit … You will receive power when the Holy Spirit comes on you; and you will be My witnesses in Jerusalem, and in all Judea and Samaria, and to the ends of the earth" (Acts 1:4-8).

Chapter 6: *Wise Leader*

Following his well-known exploits in World War I, Thomas Edward Lawrence (1888-1935), better known as Lawrence of Arabia, wrote his memoirs, which he titled *Seven Pillars of Wisdom*. The book is widely regarded as one of the finest British autobiographies of the twentieth century. Lawrence based the title on Proverbs 9:1, "Wisdom has built her house; she has hewn out its seven pillars."

T. E. Lawrence takes his seven pillars of wisdom from the most formidable leadership challenge in history, the Exodus (Exodus 18:19-23; Deuteronomy 1:13). Lawrence's seven essentials for effective leadership are wisdom, understanding, experience, ability, fear of God, trustworthiness and incorruptibility. As the title implies, the first and primary pillar of leadership is wisdom.

Webster's dictionary defines wisdom as "the faculty of making the best use of knowledge, a combination of discernment, judgment, sagacity and similar powers ... In Scripture, right judgment concerning spiritual and moral truth." The New Testament word for wisdom is *sophia*, meaning "insight into the true nature." It suggests the ability to sort through a competing set of options, and to choose the best among many good options. Wisdom is much more than knowledge, much more than the accumulation of facts—it is discernment.

The apostles looked for wisdom in those they chose to oversee the most servile tasks, such as organizing the daily distribution of food. The apostle James offered words of wisdom at the conclusion of the Jerusalem Council recorded in Acts 15. Because of a serious controversy among Church leaders over Gentile believers, the apostles called an urgent high council at headquarters, Jerusalem. While the apostles universally welcomed Gentiles into the Church, some maintained that Gentile converts must first become

Jewish proselytes. After much debate, Peter addressed the council. He reminded them how he had been responsible for the reception of Cornelius
and his family into the Church 10 years earlier. Paul and Barnabas testified
next. By simply reporting the sensational results of their ministry among
the Gentiles, they let the facts speak for themselves.

Despite the impassioned appeals of Peter, Paul and Barnabas, the strict-
er Jews held fast to their belief that adhering to the Law was required to
become Christian. With opinions firmly divided, the matter of receiving
Gentiles into the Church hung in the balance. James listened to the argu-
ments, pondered the alternatives, made a judgment and offered a word
of wisdom. He was Jesus' brother and a revered leader of the Jerusalem
Church. A hush came over the assembly when he rose. "Brothers listen
to me," James entreated. "It is my judgment … that we should not make
it difficult for the Gentiles who are turning to God. Instead we should
write to them, telling them to abstain from food polluted by idols, from
sexual immorality, from the meat of strangled animals and from blood"
(Acts 15:13, 19-20).

As with all attributes of spiritual leadership, wisdom is given by God and
cultivated by man. God's gifts are filtered through human personality and
a person's willingness to learn and improve. The spiritual leader obtains
wisdom through steadfast trust in God, earnest prayer and patient practice.

Four practical steps will aid in the spiritual leader's quest for wisdom.
Step one: listen carefully with an open mind. Suspend judgment until all
the options are considered. Step two: carefully ponder the alternatives.
Take a deep breath or two and take time to prayerfully consider the best
choice. Step three: decide. Step four: act.

God's Word has good news for the spiritual leader who seeks wisdom:
"If any of you lacks wisdom, he should ask God, who gives generously to
all without finding fault, and it will be given to him" (James 1:5).

Paul's prayer for the Christians at Colossi must constantly be on the lips
of those bearing spiritual responsibility, "asking God to fill you with the
knowledge of His will through all spiritual wisdom and understanding"
(Colossians 1:9).

Chapter 7: *Suffering Leader*

More Christians have been martyred for their faith in this past century than in all of the previous twenty combined. According to the *World Mission Digest*, in the twentieth century alone, close to 100 million Christians paid the ultimate sacrifice for Christ's cause.

The call to modern Christian leadership is an echo of the first-century call. It is a call to suffer and die. By definition, spiritual leaders must be willing to pay a much greater price than that required of their corporate or political contemporaries. "The servant-leader," writes Henri Nouwen, "is the leader who is being led to unknown, undesirable, and painful places. The way of the Christian leader is not the way of upward mobility in which our world has invested so much, but the way of downward mobility ending on the cross."[10]

The biblical requirements for servant leadership are absolute and irrevocable. "This is how we know what love is," asserts the apostle John, "Jesus Christ laid down His life for us. And we ought to lay down our lives for our brothers" (1 John 3:16). Nothing less than unconditional, radical commitment to suffer for Christ and His Church qualifies the spiritual leader.

Jesus' admonition remains the timeless benchmark for leadership: "Whoever wants to hold the first positions among you must be everybody's slave. For the Son of man did not come to be served but to serve, and to give His life as a ransom" (Mark 10:44-45, C.B. Williams).

After His Resurrection, Jesus took pains to reveal His scars. On the road to Emmaus, Jesus' followers did not recognize Him or His message. When He broke bread with them, they saw His nail-pierced hands, "Then their eyes were opened and they recognized Him" (Luke 24:31). Later that night, Jesus stood in the midst of His disciples in the upper room. "Put

your finger here; see My hands," He bade Thomas. "Reach out your hand
and put it into My side" (John 20:27). Jesus embodied the timeless truth
that scars are the marks of sterling discipleship and authentic leadership.

In April 1942, Dietrich Bonhoeffer sat in a Nazi prison awaiting his
execution, which would take place two years later. Reflecting on his suffering, he penned a letter to his twin sister, Sabine:

> **It is good to learn early that suffering and God are not a contradiction,
> but rather a unity, for the idea that God Himself is suffering, is one that
> has always been one of the most convincing teachings of Christianity.
> I think that God is nearer to suffering than to happiness, and to find
> God in this way gives peace and rest and a strong and courageous heart.**

Half a century later, Malcolm Muggeridge echoed and reaffirmed Bonhoeffer's experience and theology of suffering. In his book *A Twentieth
Century Testimony*, Muggeridge writes:

> **Contrary to what might be expected, I look back on experiences that
> at the time seemed especially desolating and painful, with particular
> satisfaction. Indeed, I can say with complete truthfulness that everything
> I have learned in my 75 years in this world, everything that has truly
> enhanced and enlightened my existence, has been through affliction and
> not through happiness, whether pursued or attained ... This of course
> is what the cross signifies, and it is the cross more than anything else,
> that has called me inexorably to Christ.**[11]

To the spiritual leader who is suffering, the apostle Paul extends words
of assurance. He validates the high cost of leadership and gives the promise of ultimate victory in Christ. "We are hard pressed on every side," the
apostle acknowledges, "but not crushed; perplexed, but not in despair;
persecuted, but not abandoned; struck down, but not destroyed ... we who
are alive are always being given over to death for Jesus' sake, so that His
life may be revealed in our mortal body" (2 Corinthians 4:8-11).

Chapter 8: *Visionary Leader*

Vision is indispensable for spiritual leadership. Leaders who powerfully and permanently influence their generation are the "seers," men and women who see deeper and farther than others. Effective leaders have a healthy discontent with the status quo. While understanding the present, "what is," the spiritual leader has a clear vision for the future, "what can be." Reality and possibility are continually held in tension.

Of course, hopes and dreams are not for leaders alone. Everyone has a dream. T. E. Lawrence said, "All men dream, but not equally. Those who dream by night in the dusty recesses of their minds awake to find that it was vanity; but the dreamers of the day are dangerous men for they may act their dreams with open eyes to make it possible."[12] Spiritual leaders turn their dreams to visions; possibility becomes passion, and passion culminates in performance.

In his biography of George W. Truett, the great Baptist leader Powhatan James wrote:

> The man of God must have insight into things spiritual. He must be able to see the mountains filled with the horses and chariots of fire; he must be able to interpret that which is written by the finger of God upon the walls of conscience; he must be able to translate the signs of the times into terms of their spiritual meaning; he must be able to draw aside, now and then, the curtain of things material and let mortals glimpse the spiritual glories which crown the mercy seat of God.[13]

Leaders see what others disregard or fail to understand. Moses, one of the greatest leaders of all time, "persevered because he saw Him who is invisible" (Hebrews 11:27). While others focused on the impossibility of an enormous task, Moses prayerfully discerned God's plan and trusted His provision. Elisha's servant saw what he thought was reality, a vast encircling army, but Elisha saw instead the victorious, invisible host of heaven (2 Kings 6:8-23). Faith gave both Moses and Elisha the right vision.

God will give the vision to those who seek and wait for it. The Lord reminded Habakkuk that "the revelation [vision] waits an appointed time … Though it linger, wait for it; it will certainly come" (Habakkuk 2:3). Once God reveals His plan, the spiritual leader must act. He or she must testify with Paul, "I was not disobedient to the vision from heaven" (Acts 26:19).

Vision involves foresight as well as insight. In addition to seeing what others fail to see, the spiritual leader's vision must go beyond his or her lifetime. The prominent twentieth-century theologian Reinhold Neibuhr avowed, "Nothing that is worth doing can be achieved in our lifetime."

The visionary leader is also an optimist, for no pessimist ever made a great leader. The spiritual leader leads with idealism and hope. The renowned bard, Robert Browning, poetically captured the essence of the optimistic leader: "One who never turned his back but marched breast forward, / Never doubted clouds would break, / Never dreamed, though right were worsted, wrong would triumph."

Above all, the spiritual leader's vision must coincide with the *Missio Dei*, God's mission. The leader must resist the counterproductive temptation to advance a personal vision. The leader's vision must be in keeping with God's mission. The mission of God in this world is to: manifest His love; reclaim and redeem His creation; exalt Christ above all; prepare the Bride (the Church) for the heavenly Bridegroom (Christ); vindicate His power and wisdom through the Church; and gather all things in heaven and earth together in Christ.

With the anonymous eighth-century hymn writer, the spiritual leader must pray:

> *Be Thou my Vision, O Lord of my heart;*
> *Naught be all else to me, save that Thou art.*
> *Thou my best thought, by day or by night,*
> *Waking or sleeping, Thy presence my light.*

Chapter 9: *Campaigning Leader*

The perennial debate over Christianity's spiritual and social mission is alive and well. The question continues to surface among leaders and followers, in boardrooms and chat rooms, in the local congregation and in the classroom: "Is our primary calling that of preaching the gospel or that of ministering to the social needs of humankind?" The answer is that God calls those whom He has ordained as spiritual leaders to proclaim the Good News to individuals *and* to campaign for each individual's well-being (John 15:16). He calls us to proclaim and campaign simultaneously! Salvation and service are not two separate missions, but rather dual aspects of the one overriding mission of fulfilling the Great Commission to "make disciples of all nations" (Matthew 28:19).

A sensitive, discerning, social conscience is at the heart of authentic discipleship. The gospel is a social gospel. John Wesley recognized and championed this. "The gospel of Christ," wrote Wesley, "knows of no religion but social, no holiness but social holiness."

In *The Seven Spirits*, published in 1907, William Booth describes the essence of what he expected from his officers (clergy).

Burning love will make the officer the true friend of mankind ... he will love the poor, the suffering, the weak, the hungry, the sick. He will go after them, and touch them, and take them by the hand. He will follow Jesus Christ's example, as described in the New Testament: "Who so hath this world's goods, and seeth his brother in need, and shuteth up his bowels of compassion from him, how dwelleth the love of God in him?"[14]

The Bible brims with accounts illustrating that proclamation and social justice are inseparable aspects of spiritual leadership. Perhaps the most significant divine encounter in the history of the Hebrew people was God's call to Moses. Startled by God in the midst of Mt. Sinai's burning bush, Moses experienced holiness and the presence of God. Then, while ready to bask in the glow of that religious experience, God called him to do a task. He was to go to the Egyptian governor and lobby for better pay, improved working conditions, fair employment practices and liberation of an oppressed people. So he went to Pharaoh declaring, "Let my people go."

False leaders bless the status quo, saying what rulers want to hear. True spiritual leaders challenge cultural and social assumptions with, "This is what the Lord says … " Amos is a good example. He admonished the leaders of the Hebrew nation to "let justice roll on like a river, righteousness like a never-failing stream!" (Amos 5:24). This continues to be the spiritual leader's dual call—justice and righteousness for all!

Jesus infuriated the religious leaders of His hometown when He adopted Isaiah's mission statement as His own. On the Sabbath day Jesus entered the synagogue in Nazareth, unrolled the scroll of the prophet Isaiah and began reading from chapter 61: "The Spirit of the Lord is on Me, because He has anointed Me to preach good news to the poor. He has sent Me to proclaim freedom for the prisoners and recovery of sight for the blind, to release the oppressed, to proclaim the year of the Lord's favor" (Luke 4:18-19).

Early Christian leaders fought against infanticide, bloody gladiator contests and human slavery. Indeed, the Church's insistence on social justice is what drew the hostility of the Roman government more than any religious issue. As Lovett Weems notes in *Leadership in the Wesleyan Spirit*, "Throughout history every tyrant from Nero to Hitler to contemporary dictators has sought first to silence the Christian Church."[15]

Working for social justice is often harder than preaching the Good News. It takes grit and fortitude. Of Florence Nightingale, Lytton Strachey wrote:

> **It was not by gentle sweetness and womanly self-abnegation that she brought order out of chaos in the Scutari Hospitals, that from her own resources she had clothed the British Army, that she had spread her dominion over the serried and reluctant powers of the official world; it**

was by strict method, by stern discipline, by rigid attention to detail, by ceaseless labor, by fixed determination of the indomitable will. Beneath her cool and calm demeanor, there lurked fierce and passionate fires.[16]

Oh that in the heart of every spiritual leader may "lurk fierce and passionate fires" for truth and justice. May we remember our Lord's words: "I tell you the truth, whatever you did for one of the least of these brothers of Mine, you did for Me" (Matthew 25:40).

Chapter 10: *Humble Leader*

I n his acclaimed book, *Leadership is an Art,* Max De Pree identifies the essence of what he terms artful leadership: "The first responsibility of a leader is to define reality. The last is to say thank you. In between the two, the leader must become a servant and a debtor. That sums up the progress of an artful leader."[17] It is the interminable time between "defining reality" and "saying thank you" that presents the greatest challenge and privilege of leadership. Confirmation of outstanding, productive leadership principally comes from the leader's followers—those whom the leader serves and those to whom the leader is indebted. Followers have affirmed the leader if they are reaching their potential, growing and learning, serving others, achieving required results, managing conflict and becoming flexible with grace.

Finding fulfillment in others' accomplishments is the foundation of spiritual leadership. Such leadership opposes that of leaders who only find fulfillment in personal accomplishment. The practice of the Christian faith requires the exact opposite of wielding authority. Faith is essentially an act of submission to the Lordship of Christ and obedience to Him. Therefore, however much spiritual leaders are required to speak and act authoritatively in the name of Christ, their Christian identity must remain that of a servant. As the apostle Paul modeled, the spiritual leader must be fundamentally identified as *doulos,* a slave of Christ (Romans 1:1). The leader who exercises authority all of the time has little time to humbly practice obedience.

The word "humility" piqued my understanding in the context of leadership when Jim Collins commented on it in his groundbreaking 2001 volume entitled *Good to Great: Why Some Companies Make the Leap ... and*

Others Don't. Collins examines companies that went from good to great. Among the many characteristics separating these companies from others is that they all had what he terms a "Level 5 leader." Collins defines Level 5 leaders as those who direct their ego away from themselves to the larger goal of leading their company to greatness. These leaders are men and women of a "complex, paradoxical mix of intense professional will and extreme personal humility." They are leaders who create outstanding results but avoid public praise. They are never impressed by their self-importance.

In his book *Serious Call*, the eighteenth-century Christian mystic William Law describes the character of genuine servant leadership:

> Let every day be a day of humility; condescend to all the weaknesses and infirmities of your fellow-creatures, cover their frailties, love their excellencies, encourage their virtues, relieve their wants, rejoice in their prosperities, compassionate their distress, receive their friendship, overlook their unkindness, forgive their malice, be a servant of servants, and condescend to do the lowliest offices of the lowest of mankind.[18]

Paul, arguably the sharpest intellectual and most fervent evangelist of all the apostles, acknowledged, "I am the least of the apostles and do not even deserve to be called an apostle" (1 Corinthians 15:9). Later, he declared, "I am the least of all God's people" (Ephesians 3:8). In his final days, he affirmed, "Christ Jesus came into the world to save sinners—of whom I am the worst" (1 Timothy 1:15).

By definition, leaders must have followers. A leader without willing followers is a contradiction. I say "willing followers" because having appointed followers but not willing followers is possible. It happens. Authentic leaders engender willing, loyal followers. The servant leader earns the respect and trust of everyone who is a follower. Peter F. Drucker, well-known author and lecturer on leadership, writes: "The final requirement of effective leadership is to earn trust. Otherwise there will not be any followers—and the only definition of a leader is someone who has followers."[19]

While the spiritual leader defines success according to the achievements his or her followers, at the same time the leader carries the awesome weight of responsibility. Effective leaders are rarely permissive. However, when things go wrong they do not blame others. It is the weak, insecure leader who consistently blames others for failure. Blaming others is thinly disguised egotism.

As John Keats, the much-admired English poet, noted: "He who discommendeth others, overtly commendeth himself." The spiritual leader who takes ultimate responsibility does not feel intimidated by coworkers' strength. An effective leader always wants to be surrounded by strong colleagues. The weak, ineffective leader prefers to purge staff of those who are stronger. Invariably, the consequence of such a policy is ineffective, counterproductive and failed leadership.

Edward Koch, the popular, uninhibited, former mayor of New York City, was known for asking one question of people he met on the streets. He would shake hands with his constituents, look them squarely in the eye and with a broad smile ask, "How am I doing?" It was an inspired political tactic, but the mayor really sought the truth from his citizens. While he often received compliments, he was more interested in the criticism. Mayor Koch understood that, between defining the reality of leading a major world city and saying "thank you" to his supporters, he was primarily a servant of, and a debtor to, his followers.

When you go to your place of work tomorrow, ask one of your trusted followers, "How am I doing?" Then listen carefully.

Chapter 11: *Influential Leader*

L eadership is influence. Essentially, it is the ability of one person to persuade and motivate others. A leader can lead only as far as he or she can influence. Of all the biblical examples of influential spiritual leadership, Peter stands out as a natural. His leadership was spontaneous and unquestioned. What Peter did, the others did. Where Peter went, the others went. When Peter said, "I am going out to fish," his friends replied, "We'll go with you" (John 21:3).

In 1 Peter 5:1-7, the disciple Jesus commissioned to lead His fledgling Church provides succinct and definitive lessons on spiritual leadership. Samuel Logan Brengle reflects on this instructive passage in his book, *Ancient Prophets:*

> [In the words] of Peter: "The elders which are among you I exhort … Feed the flock of God … not by constraint, but willingly; not for filthy lucre [or rank or power], but a ready mind; neither as being lords over God's heritage, but being examples to the flock … Likewise, ye younger, submit yourselves unto the elder. Yea, all of you be subject to one another, and be clothed with humility." Nothing will so surely insure [our] prosperous and happy future … as this spirit, and I am persuaded that nothing other than this can insure it.[20]

Few passages express more clearly the importance of leaders (elders) in the early Church than this one. Through a series of contrasts, Peter establishes the perils and the privileges of spiritual leadership. The spiritual leader is to accept the office not under coercion, but willingly; not to make a disgraceful profit, but be eager to serve; not to be a petty dictator, but to be the shepherd and the example of the flock. Peter echoes what Jesus said to His ambitious disciples: "You know that those who are regarded as rulers of the Gentiles lord it over them, and their high officials exercise authority over them. Not so with you. Instead, whoever wants to become great among you must be your servant, and whoever wants to be first must be slave of all" (Mark 10:42-44).

Peter first addresses the leader's motivation, saying, "Be shepherds of God's flock … not because you must, but because you are willing, as God wants you to be" (1 Peter 5:2). The servant leader must assume responsibility gladly, not under compulsion. It is God who calls. The response must echo that of the prophet Isaiah, "Here am I. Send me!" (Isaiah 6:8).

Of all temptations, spiritual leaders must continually guard against the allure of personal gain, financial or otherwise. Greed is insidious and insatiable. Monetary greed is not the only component of the Greek phrase translated "filthy lucre" (KJV), "shameful gain" (RSV) or "greedy for money" (NIV). The phrase can also apply to greed for popularity or power. For spiritual leaders, prestige and power are greater temptations than money.

While sanctified ambition can provide positive motivation, if not kept in perspective by the Holy Spirit it can quickly degenerate to intolerance. Illustrations of the deterioration of ambition are plentiful. Most readers can provide personal illustrations of encounters with ambitious leaders.

The leader must set a worthy example. Peter reminds the elders of the spirit in which their leadership is to be exercised, the spirit of the Chief Shepherd. As "under shepherd" the spiritual leader must act in concert with the Chief Shepherd, indeed, the Good Shepherd (John 10:11-15). As the distinguished English Baptist preacher, Charles Haddon Spurgeon, commented, "Ministers may do more by their example than by their discourses."[21]

Peter lists humility as the concluding requisite for spiritual leadership. While humility was discussed in the previous chapter, influence and humility are interconnected. The influential spiritual leader is "clothed with humility." Peter counsels, "clothe yourselves with humility toward one another, because, 'God opposes the proud but gives favor to the humble.' Humble yourselves, therefore, under God's mighty hand, that he may lift you up in due time" (1 Peter 5:5-6). The Greek word for "clothed" occurs only three times in the New Testament. It specifically refers to the long white apron worn by slaves. Peter reminds his fellow elders that spiritual leaders are to stand "aproned" with humility, ready to serve in the name of Christ. The spiritual leader must accept the splendid responsibility to love, nurture and influence his or her followers, "clothed with humility toward one another."

Chapter 12: *Cheerful Leader*

Joy is one of the most common words in the New Testament. Jesus declared that the goal of His teaching was "that My joy may be in you and that your joy may be complete" (John 15:11). From his prison cell, the apostle Paul echoed this life principle. He urged believers to, "Rejoice in the Lord always" (Philippians 4:4).

Joy triggers physical, as well as spiritual, well-being. According to Proverbs 17:22, "A cheerful heart is good medicine, but a crushed spirit dries up the bones." In his highly praised book, *Laughter Joy and Healing,* Donald Demaray describes laughing as "internal jogging." He states that "humor sends pleasure coursing through our thought processes, assists in reestablishing perspective, opens our minds to new vistas of reality, and releases us from tension."[22]

Humor is not only good medicine for the soul and body; it is essential for effective spiritual leadership. In his helpful, practical book, *Christian Leadership,* A.E. Norrish draws on his years of missionary service to India. Concerning humor, he recalls:

> **I have never met leadership without a sense of humor, this ability to stand outside oneself and one's circumstances, to see things in perspective and laugh. It is a great safety valve! You will never lead others far without the joy of the Lord and its concomitant, a sense of humor.**[23]

Even the distinguished, somber German theologian, Helmut Thielicke, recognized the value of humor. Reflecting on the ministry and leadership of the popular nineteenth-century British preacher, Charles Haddon Spurgeon, Thielicke remarked:

Should we not see that lines of laughter about the eyes are just as much marks of faith as are the lines of care and seriousness? Is it only earnestness that is baptized? Is laughter pagan? We have already allowed too much that is good to be lost to the Church and cast many pearls before swine. A church is in a bad way when it banishes laughter from the sanctuary and leaves it to the cabaret, the nightclub and the toastmasters.[24]

God made man in His image; therefore, man's sense of humor is a gift from his Creator. As with all other God-given gifts, humor must be cultivated. If used wisely, humor is of inestimable value to the spiritual leader, both for what it does personally and its enhancement to ministry.

When humor dissipates, followers stiffen. One of the ever-present pitfalls of leadership is the tendency for leaders to take themselves too seriously, presuming that everything depends upon the person in charge. Spiritual leaders must heed the "still small voice" that bids them, "relax, you're only human!" Leaders secure enough to laugh at their own short-comings will ease tense situations, engender confidence and quickly move on to fulfilling mission. The spiritual leader relies on the promise that "the joy of the Lord is your strength" (Nehemiah 8:10).

As a divisional youth secretary (or regional youth minister), I learned a memorable, vivid lesson from an unlikely source. While attending a camping convention, I listened to a motivational speaker tell leaders to lighten up. "If you are tempted to take yourself too seriously," challenged the presenter, "go back to your hotel room alone. Stand in front of the full-length mirror. Remove all your clothes, and contemplate what you see. If after taking a good, long look, you still take yourself too seriously, jump up and down!" While I did not undertake the suggested exercise (the mental image was enough), I have never forgotten the point.

The Bible reminds us that, "There is a time … to weep and a time to laugh" (Ecclesiastes 3:4). As spiritual leaders, we must wisely model the balance between tears and laughter—between solemnity and humor. Give it a try right now! May I hear that laugh, or at least see a smile?

Chapter 13: *Tempted Leader*

Every profession comes with certain occupational hazards. The spiritual leader faces unique and sometimes subtle pitfalls that are often temptations of the spirit as well as the flesh. The rise to leadership can breed shrewd pride that, if unchecked, will eventually disqualify the leader from further responsibilities. God's Word is clear on the subject: "The Lord detests all the proud of heart. Be sure of this: They will not go unpunished ... Pride goes before destruction, a haughty spirit before a fall" (Proverbs 16:5,18).

In *Spiritual Leadership: A Commitment to Excellence for Every Believer,* J. Oswald Sanders offers three tests to discover whether a leader has succumbed to the sin of pride:[25]

First is the test of precedence: How do we react when another is selected for the assignment we expected, or the office we coveted? Second is the test of sincerity: In our moments of honest self-criticism we will say many things about ourselves, and really mean them. But how do we feel when others, especially our rivals, say exactly the same things about us? Third is the test of criticism: Does criticism arouse hostility and resentment in our hearts, and cause us to fly to immediate self-justification? Do we hasten to lash out at the critic?

Pride and popularity go hand in hand. When either flourishes, the need for the other develops. Pride nurtures the desire to be popular, and popularity can easily become the footing for pride. People are generally drawn to Christ through another person. Personality plays a key role in evangelism. This is not new; it was as typical in the early Church as it is today. Spiritual leaders, however, must guard against the intoxication of popularity, constantly striving to transfer attention and allegiance from the leader to Christ. As with John the Baptist, the leader must affirm, "He must become greater; I must become less." The revered British preacher Charles Haddon Spurgeon cautioned:

> **Success exposes a man to the pressure of people and thus tempts him to hold on to his gains by means of fleshly methods and practices … Success can go to my head, and will unless I remember that it is God who accomplishes the work, that He can continue to do so without my help, and that He will be able to make out with other means whenever He cuts me down to size.**[26]

Following closely on the heels of pride and popularity is the temptation to seek higher position. Always striving for the next level of leadership brings about noticeable changes in personality. How often we hear or say, "He was so___ until he became___," or, "Since her new appointment she has changed." It is counterproductive to authentic, effective leadership when position defines personality, when assignment affects attitude, when station alters self.

Throughout history, effective spiritual leaders have been men and women who refuse to take themselves too seriously. They possess a healthy self-awareness that checks the subtle temptations that issue from pride, popularity and position. If unchecked, temptations can become more sinister, harder to control and hurtful to others. Among a long list of temptations, the spiritual leader must constantly avoid abusing power, sexual enticements and exploiting people for personal gain.

As to how spiritual leaders overcome temptation, the answer is in God's Word. James 4:7 reassures: "Submit yourselves, then, to God. Resist the devil, and he will flee from you."

Chapter 14: *Incorruptible Leader*

Towards the end of 2013, a national Gallup poll asked, "How you would rate the honesty and ethical standards of people in these different fields: very high, high, average, low or very low?" Nurses were rated very high or high by 82% of those polled. Clergy were rated very high or high by a record low of 47%. This was the first time this rating has dropped below 50% since Gallup first asked about clergy in 1977. Clergy have historically ranked near the top among professions, but the rating has declined steadily since the 1977 poll.[27]

For two millennia the Church has been telling the world to admit to its sins, repent and believe the gospel. Today, the world is telling the Church to face up to her sins, repent and start being the true Church of the gospel.

"One of the universal cravings of our times," contends Commissioner James Osborne, past National Commander of The Salvation Army USA in an address delivered at the International Conference of Leaders in 1988, "is a hunger for compelling and creative leadership. The scarcest resource in the world ... is solid, dependable, loyal, strong leadership." The word integrity captures these requisite qualities.

Integrity is the word for our day. While cultures may define it differently, it essentially means keeping our promises, doing what we say we will do, being accountable for our actions. Integrity is required for spiritual leadership. It is the inward foundational source of all leadership qualities. Listen once again to Jethro's advice to his son-in-law to appoint trustworthy men to assist Moses in the vast administration of the children of Israel in their journey to the Promised Land. "Listen now to me, and I will give you some advice," Jethro entreated, "select capable men from all the people—men who fear God, trustworthy men who hate dishonest gain—and appoint them as officials over thousands, hundreds, fifties and tens" (Exodus 18:19-21).

Authentic spiritual leadership relates more to inward character than outward performance. As Oliver Wendell Homes put it, "What lies behind us and what lies before us are tiny matters compared to what lies within us."

One of the most revered presidents of the United States was Abraham Lincoln. His enduring legacy is rooted in his character. Lincoln was fair, trustworthy, sincere, straightforward, of high moral principle and truthful, hence his nickname, "Honest Abe." In short, he was a man of integrity. In his acclaimed book, *Lincoln on Leadership—Executive Strategies for Tough Times*, Donald Phillips writes: "Even though he had some detractors, Lincoln attained success, admiration, and a positive image by maintaining his integrity and honesty. Those who questioned his upbringing and education, or even his political affiliations, tended not to doubt his integrity."[28] Phillips goes on to list Abraham Lincoln's principles for leadership, all of which are rooted in his character, and which serve as guideposts for genuine spiritual leadership:

- Give your subordinates a fair chance with equal freedom and opportunity for success.
- When you make it to the top, turn and reach down for the person behind you.
- Set, and respond to, fundamental goals and values that move your followers.
- Be consistently fair and decent, in both business and personal matters.
- Stand with anybody who stands right. Stand with him while he is right and part with him when he goes wrong.
- Never add the weight of your character to a charge against a person without knowing it to be true.
- Advance the aims of the organization and also help those who serve it.
- If you once forfeit the confidence of your fellow citizens, you can never regain their respect and esteem.

"Integrity" comes from the Latin *integritas,* meaning wholeness, entireness and completeness. The root word is *integer*, which means untouched, intact and entire. The spiritual leader's life must be rooted in integrity, that is, not divided (duplicity) or merely pretending (hypocrisy).

The Old Testament Hebrew word for "integrity" is *thom*. It connotes "wholeness" and "completeness" and is thus often translated as "integrity." The plural, *thummin*, refers to the part of the ceremonial apparel worn only by the high priest. The *Thummin* represented the perfection—the pure integrity—that is required to stand before God and discern His will. (See a fuller description of the *Urim* and the *Thummin* in Chapter 22, page 66.)

After four decades of occupying various leadership responsibilities, I can attest to the importance of integrity in all areas of life and leadership. The most difficult decisions invariably affect the lives of others, and in many instances, this includes their families and wider community. I have faced countless complicated and problematic situations, where no win-win solution could be found. In such circumstances, the answer is only discovered through intense prayer, consideration of all aspects of the matter, reaching a fair and firm decision and finally courageously taking action. Spiritual leaders must affirm with Job: "Till I die, I will not deny my integrity. I will maintain my righteousness and never let go of it; my conscience will not reproach me as long as I live" (Job 27:5-6).

Chapter 15: *Self-disciplined Leader*

Ralph Waldo Emerson often greeted old friends whom he had not seen in a while with the salutation, "What's become clear to you since we last met?" The more I ponder the subject of leadership, the more it becomes clear to me that effective spiritual leadership results from a dynamic combination of gift and grit, skill and sweat, innate ability and intense work.

Spiritual leaders are both born and made. One is born to be a leader in the sense that God endows leaders with gifts that uniquely equip them for special tasks. Without question, some leaders are born with personalities and qualities that allow them to take up leadership responsibilities more readily than others. Often these traits can be identified at a young age. However, it is discipline, learning and growth that are crucial to becoming a spiritual leader.

As with Jeremiah, God declares to each of His chosen leaders: "Before I formed you in the womb I knew you, before you were born I set you apart" (Jeremiah 1:5). Every minister of the gospel who is chosen and ordained by God rests in the grand assurance of a God-sent leader. Jesus reminds all His disciples: "You did not choose Me, but I chose you and appointed you to go and bear fruit—fruit that will last. Then the Father will give you whatever you ask in My name" (John 15:16).

In addition to this indispensable divine ordination, effective spiritual leaders are those who develop their God-given gifts through devotion and self-discipline. Discipline is the quality that separates the exceptional from the acceptable leader. In the vernacular, discipline "separates the men from the boys and the women from the girls." Paul reminded his young protégé, Timothy, to concentrate on the disciplines of leadership: "If anyone sets his heart on being an overseer, he desires a noble task. Now the overseer must be above reproach, the husband of but one wife, temperate, self-controlled, respectable, hospitable, able to teach, not given to drunkenness, not violent but gentle, not quarrelsome, not a lover of money" (1 Timothy 3:2).

In *The Seven Habits of Highly Effective People,* Stephen Covey lists as his third habit "Put first things first." Covey explains that "discipline derives from *disciple*—disciple to a philosophy, disciple to a set of principles, disciple to a set of values, disciple to an overriding purpose, to a superordinate goal or a person who represents that goal … If you are an effective manager of your self, your discipline comes from within; it is a function of your independent will."[29] If this is true for secular leadership, it is even truer for the servant-leader disciple of Christ.

The spiritual leader is able to lead others only when the self has been conquered. In *Spiritual Leadership,* J. Oswald Sanders observes:

> **Only the disciplined person will rise to his highest powers. The leader is able to lead others because he has conquered himself … A leader is a person who has first submitted willingly and learned to obey a discipline imposed from without, but who then imposes on himself a much more rigorous discipline from within. Those who rebel against authority and scorn self-discipline seldom qualify for leadership of a high order … [Those] of leadership caliber will work while others waste time, study while others sleep and pray while others play."[30]**

The eighteenth-century preacher and evangelist George Whitefield was a man of discipline. He usually arose at four o'clock in the morning, and he was equally punctual in retiring at night. His friends confirmed that as the clock struck 10 each evening, no matter how many guests were in his home or in spite of the most interesting, animated discussion, Reverend Whitefield would rise from his chair, walk toward the door, and with a good-natured smile and gesture say, "Come, my friends, it is time for all good folks to be at home."[31]

As disciples of Jesus, as soldiers called to ministry, as twenty-first-century spiritual leaders, let us adopt Amy Carmichael's prayer for discipline:

God, harden me against myself,
The coward with pathetic voice
Who craves for ease and rest and joy.
Myself, arch-traitor to myself,
My hollowest friend,
My deadliest foe,
My clog, whatever road I go.

Discipline is the heart of discipleship and the foundation for effective spiritual leadership. While discipline has a wide variety of meanings—from correction and punishment to a field of study in school—the root meaning is "an orderly, prescribed conduct or pattern of behavior." In short, it means self-control. From making sure that "your feet hit the floor" when the alarm rings in the morning, to persevering towards a long-term goal, discipline equips and empowers the leader to achieve a vision.

In her address delivered during the 2004 International Conference of Leaders, Commissioner Christine MacMillan, then-Territorial Commander of the Canada and Bermuda Territory, reminded her colleagues that "vision and passion without perseverance results in unproductive leadership." Productive leaders persist when others give up.

In her book, *Jesus, CEO*, Laurie Beth Jones encourages spiritual leaders to practice the "WOWSE model." Every time a leader feels rejected and is tempted to be discouraged, he or she should say, quietly, "WOWSE!" The acronym means "With or Without Someone Else." When she was building her company, she would often affirm, "I will build this company with or without someone else." While spiritual leadership requires vision and passion, you will never reach a goal without discipline and perseverance. With the apostle Paul, the spiritual leader must "press on toward the goal to win the prize for which God has called me heavenward in Christ Jesus" (Philippians 3:14).

God offers wisdom to leaders who seek it through ardent prayer and passionate discipline. Solomon, to whom God granted his prayer for wisdom, introduces the book of Proverbs with the clear purpose and theme:

"The proverbs of Solomon son of David, king of Israel: for attaining wisdom and discipline; for understanding words of insight; for acquiring a disciplined and prudent life, doing what is right and just and fair" (Proverbs 1:1-3). Several verses later Solomon succinctly states his theme: "The fear of the Lord is the beginning of knowledge, but fools despise wisdom and discipline" (Proverbs 1:7).

The wise leader of the Proverbs seeks knowledge, commits to understanding what is studied and applies those lessons to life and leadership. The disciplined leader strives to live a life of carefully chosen words, concern for others, and love of God.

The foolish leader, on the other hand, has no desire to learn, no desire to change and, in the end, no desire for God. An undisciplined leader is a contradiction in terms. Such a leader soon becomes known for folly rather than wisdom.

Solomon's lesson is especially crucial for young leaders. The discipline learned and habits cultivated in the first years of ministry will last a lifetime. The most important year in the life of a spiritual leader is the first year. The discipline of the early days of ministry establishes the pattern for life.

Jesus remains the ultimate example of disciplined leadership. He could repeat His mission statement at any moment, and He never diverged from it: "I have come that they may have life, and have it to the full" (John 10:10).

I know of few people more disciplined than my highly respected and beloved wife, Marilyn. Before even her morning cup of tea, she is on her knees and in the Word. She urges family, friends and all who will listen to live each day by the four Ds of triumphant discipleship; "Live each day," she challenges, "with Discipline, Diligence, Dignity and Daring."

Chapter 16: *Risk-taking Leader*

In my early years of ministry, a friend of mine taught me how to play a new board game, Risk. The game has become a family holiday standard. Its extravagant objective is to conquer the world. Each player begins with a few armies that are carefully and (hopefully) strategically placed in countries on the board's map. Risking one's military strength against competing armies achieves victory. The roll of the dice determines the risk. Although I contend that my worthy opponent of 30-plus years ago would frequently change the rules of engagement to meet his scheming ends, I enjoyed the vicarious thrill of risking all to achieve world domination, a goal that on the Risk board I rarely achieved.

In the real world, risk is less appealing and carries the potential for profound consequences. Every great leader, however, must take risks. If a leader is to navigate followers through uncharted waters to places no one has gone before, taking risks is essential.

In their popular book *The Leadership Challenge,* James Kouzes and Barry Posner describe leaders as pioneers, as opposed to settlers: "Leaders are pioneers—people who are willing to step out into the unknown. They are people who are willing to take risks, to innovate and experiment in order to find new and better ways of doing things."[32] Leaders look beyond what "is" and envision what "can be." There is only way to move from "what is" (reality) to "what can be" (potential)—take risks. Joel Barker also uses the metaphors of pioneers and settlers to characterize the risk-taking leader. He notes:

What's the difference between a pioneer and a settler? It is the settler who always is calling toward the horizon, "Is it safe out there now?" The voice calling back, "Of course it's safe out here!" is the pioneer's. That

is because the pioneers take the risk, go out early, and make the new territory safe.[33]

Doug Murren observes: "All paradigm pioneers have a different spirit from the naysayers about them. They have the ability to see a new thing, to perceive a bright future, to tap into the power of God."[34] The great spiritual leaders in the Bible—Moses, Joshua, David, Peter and Paul—were models of "pioneer" leadership. (Jesus, of course, was the ultimate pioneer.) They consistently ignored the naysayer, looked to the spiritual horizon, tapped into God's power and, by faith, moved ahead.

Hebrews 11:1 defines faith as "being sure of what we hope for and certain of what we do not see." The writer of Hebrews goes on to record the honor roll of faith, the risk-takers who trusted God, envisioned His solution and accomplished what others deemed impossible. Abraham became the "Father of God's people" because he trusted God and took the risk of leaving his homeland to follow God's instruction (Hebrews 11:8-19). Moses' parents risked their own lives as they "hid him for three months after he was born ... [for] they were not afraid of the king's edict" (Hebrews 11:23). Moses risked his identity and life when he "refused to be known as the son of Pharaoh's daughter" (Hebrews 11:24-28). Rahab, the prostitute and direct ancestor of Jesus, risked her life "because she welcomed the spies, was not killed with those who were disobedient" (Hebrews 11:31). This magnificent chapter makes it clear that God's people have the capacity to be visionary, risk-taking pioneers. We call them spiritual leaders.

To some degree all leaders have a natural aversion to taking risks to accomplish change, especially when things are going well. Spiritual leaders must remind themselves that they serve a God who declares, "I am making everything new!" (Revelation 21:5). God is not concerned with keeping the status quo. From the beginning, God has been making a new order of creation. As God's agent for change, the spiritual leader must take the inherent risks of leadership. Whatever the challenge you face today, take the risk. Go for it!

Chapter 17: *Courageous Leader*

Courage is an essential characteristic of effective spiritual leadership. The apostle Paul challenged the church leaders in Corinth to "Be on your guard; stand firm in the faith; be men of courage; be strong" (1 Corinthians 16:13).

Every leader must have the courage to make difficult decisions even in the face of fear. In moments of fear, the leader must claim the sure promise that "God has not given us a spirit of fear, but of power and of love and of a sound mind" (2 Timothy 1:7).

Mark Twain noted, "Courage is the mastery of fear, not the absence of fear." Fear and courage are in reality, partners. David Ben-Gurion, the famed freedom fighter and first prime minister of Israel, stated, "Courage is a special kind of knowledge: the knowledge of how to fear what ought to be feared and how not to fear what ought not to be feared." The distinguished theologian, Karl Barth, said it best: "Courage is fear that has said its prayers."

Great leaders have one indispensable and defining trait in common. Each has faced overwhelming challenges with determined courage: from Helen Keller (1880-1968), who overcame dual disabilities of deafness and blindness to become a champion of those stricken with these afflictions, to Malala Yousafzai (1997-), a Pakistani schoolgirl who survived an attack from the Taliban and defied overwhelming persecution to become an international advocate for human rights, women's rights and the right to education.

From William Wilberforce (1759-1833), a leader of the campaign against slavery in Great Britain who lived to see the passage of the Slavery Abolition Act of 1833, to Martin Luther King (1929-1968) who symbolized the fight against racial discrimination in the U.S., to Nelson Mandela (1918-2013), who courageously fought the discriminatory system of apartheid in South Africa during more than 20 years of imprisonment.

From Dietrich Bonhoeffer (1906-1945)—a successful German Lutheran pastor who became an outspoken critic against the atrocities of Nazism in Germany, and who refused opportunities to leave Germany permanently, courageously stayed in the country of his birth and was eventually arrested and executed in Flossenberg concentration camp in 1945—to Mother Teresa (1910-1997), who left her Albanian home for India with virtually no money and devoted her life to serving the poor of Calcutta, overcoming poverty, disease and criticism. She expanded her mission to support the poor and disadvantaged across the world.

The indispensable quality that all of these agents of change shared and that all spiritual leaders must share is courage.

After Moses' death, God chose Joshua to lead His people into the Promised Land. As newly appointed leader of the largest encampment in history, Joshua set out to guide the children of Israel across the Jordan River and into the Promised Land. The task was enormous. Joshua faced a crisis in his leadership role. He had to contend with superior military powers in the Promised Land, while at the same time facing them with an untrained and undisciplined band of nomadic shepherds, who were born in the wilderness and unaccustomed to fighting. As he camped with his followers on the banks of the Jordan River, Joshua received God's command:

> Be strong and courageous, because you will lead these people to inherit the land I swore to their forefathers to give them. Be strong and very courageous. Be careful to obey all the law my servant Moses gave you; do not turn from it to the right or to the left, that you may be successful wherever you go ... Have I not commanded you? Be strong and courageous. Do not be terrified; do not be discouraged, for the Lord your God will be with you wherever you go (Joshua 1:6-9).

In a world in turmoil, the spiritual leader must face his or her fears, look to the Lord for strength and direction and then courageously act. Today, more than ever, a confused, frustrated, discouraged and tired world pleads for spiritual leaders of courage—men and women who will conquer fear and act in the name of Christ. To become the courageous leader God intends, spiritual leaders must follow Paul's admonition to the Church at Ephesus:

> **Put on the full armor of God so that you can take your stand against the devil's schemes. For our struggle is not against flesh and blood, but against the rulers, against the authorities, against the powers of this dark world and against the spiritual forces of evil in the heavenly realms. Therefore, put on the full armor of God, so that when the day of evil comes, you may be able to stand your ground, and after you have done everything, to stand (Ephesians 6:11-13).**

Take the challenge today. Do something courageous in the name of Christ.

Chapter 18: *Situational Leader*

New Games, an innovative camp athletic program for children, swept the world of resident camping in the late 1970s. The admirable goal of each game was to minimize competition and maximize fun. Activities commenced with the leader robustly affirming the motto, "Play Hard—Play Fair—Nobody Hurt." Games concluded with an equally triumphant declaration that every participant was a winner. New Games never produced losers! While the New Games fad has waned, I have often wished that the "rules of leadership" could be as simple and produce similar results. Think of it: a strategy that would encourage hard work, treat everyone fairly and in the process everyone would be happy and no one would get hurt. Most important of all, everyone would win! Oh, if it were only possible to develop New Leadership Games—innovative leadership methods that would follow simple rules and ensure positive, dramatic outcomes. While the variables and dynamics of leadership are far removed from child's play, New Games' guiding principles are truly at the heart of servant leadership. First-class leaders persistently strive to "lead hard" with energy and enthusiasm. They "lead fair" with compassion and consistency. They make every effort to ensure that "no one is hurt" with sensitivity and caring.

Of the three principles, "leading hard" is the easiest to achieve. Leaders typically work hard. Avoiding hurt is most difficult to consistently accomplish. Every leader has tales of heartbreaking "battlefield casualties." However, a spiritual leader's greatest challenge is treating everyone fairly, while at the same time recognizing each follower's unique abilities and needs. The sincere endeavor to treat everyone fairly can easily deteriorate into treating everyone in the same manner. This inflexible approach results in frustrated leaders and followers. While effective leadership requires the fair treatment of everyone, it is essential that every follower be guided individually. Spiritual leaders must intentionally practice situational leadership.

We define situational leadership as leadership that matches the style of leadership to the situation or to the followers. There is no one best leadership style. Different situations call for different leadership styles. Each situation involves a complex mixture of diverse personalities, interest levels, skills and motivation.

Phillip V. Lewis, in his groundbreaking book *Transformational Leadership,* notes that Jesus remains the classic example of a situational leader:[35]

> **[Jesus] was autocratic with those who would turn His "Father's house into a market" (John 2:13-16), but welcomed little children (Mark 10:13-16). He loved and understood the rich young ruler (Mark 10:17-25). He was a servant-leader with His disciples (John 13:1-17), but He judged and condemned the teachers of the Law and the Pharisees (Matthew 23).**

Jesus adjusted his leadership style to meet each situation. While His style was flexible, His purpose remained the same. His goal was to do God's will by bringing in the Kingdom (John 6:35-40; Matthew 16:13-19).

As K. G. Prunty states, "Jesus was a determined leader whose very character was like granite. He was at times compassionate and tender and at other times furious with the status quo. The poor and powerless stirred the deepest mercy in Him. The rich and the powerful religious could arouse His consternation and anger."[36] Becoming a situational leader starts with recognizing that followers approach their tasks differently. In *The Situational Leader,* Dr. Paul Hersey divides followers into four categories, those who are:[37]

1. Unable and unwilling
2. Unable but willing
3. Able but unwilling
4. Able and willing

Just as followers fall into one of four categories, leaders, too, tend to lead in one of four categories. Every leader feels more comfortable and successful in one of four groupings:

1. Telling
2. Selling
3. Participating
4. Delegating

The goal is to apply the correct leadership style to the follower's style or situation. Each of the four types of followers needs a matching style of leadership:

1. "Unable and unwilling" followers need "telling" leadership—a leader who provides specific instructions and closely supervises performance.
2. "Unable but willing" followers call for "selling" leadership—a leader who clearly explains decisions and provides opportunity for clarification.
3. "Able but unwilling" followers need "participating" leadership—a leader who shares ideas and facilitates followers in decision-making.
4. "Able and willing" followers work best with "delegating" leadership—a leader who happily turns over responsibility for making decisions and implementation.

Spiritual leaders strive to employ all four leadership styles to best meet the needs of their individual followers. While a leader feels most comfortable in one of the leadership categories, he or she will need to practice the other three styles in order to effectively lead followers that best respond to those styles.

The apostle Paul provides the never-ending leadership challenge. He practiced situational leadership. He was committed to doing whatever was necessary in a given situation to reach his ultimate goal. With Paul, may we declare, "To the weak I became weak, to win the weak. I have be-

come all things to all men so that by all possible means I might save some"
(1 Corinthians 9:22).

Chapter 19: *Team Leader*

In 550 B.C., the Chinese philosopher Lao-Tzu defined the essence of effective leadership. The sage declared, "A leader is best when people barely know he exists. Not so good when people obey and acclaim him. Worse when they despise him. But of a good leader who talks little when his work is done, his aim fulfilled, they will say, 'We did it ourselves.'"

The challenge for twenty-first-century leaders is to understand and model this axiom. The concept is more easily understood than practiced. While most readers will say "Amen" to the principle, considerably fewer will model it.

An interesting dilemma exists in The Salvation Army's military structure that affords the movement remarkable advantages. With commission and command, William Booth efficiently and effectively spread the Army's mission around the world. A stroke of the pen and young, dedicated, obedient officers were ordered to the far reaches of the globe. When it comes to deploying soul-saving troops and taking swift decisive action in the field, the Army's structure is ideal for the task. When it comes to team ministry, however, the mission's military structure presents significant challenges.

Military structure and its accompanying nomenclature better serves authoritarian rather than collaborative leadership. While leaders must at times make unilateral, unpopular and lonely decisions, every effort should be made to approach challenges and decisions in collaboration with the leadership team. Gone are the days when, without team support, a leader can say, "Do it!" and it is done.

Leadership is one of the 20 spiritual gifts revealed in the New Testament. A complete list of spiritual gifts is compiled by combining the gifts mentioned in Romans 12:6-8, 1 Corinthians 12:4-11, 28 and Ephesians 4:11-12. In many contemporary translations the original word for "leadership" is *proistamenos,* which literally means "giving aid; becoming a protector or guardian." The Greek word is translated differently in various versions of the Bible. For example, the King James Version uses the word "ruleth," the J.B. Phillips Paraphrase uses the phrase "the man who wields authority." The Revised Standard Version stays close to the heart of the meaning, with the translation "he who gives aid."

The New Testament model for servant leadership is giving aid, comfort, direction and protection to those in the leader's care. It is the picture of the shepherd, not the monarch. As Henri Nouwen notes:

When Jesus speaks about shepherding, He does not want us to think about a brave, lonely shepherd who takes care of a large flock of obedient sheep. In many ways, He makes it clear that ministry is a communal and mutual experience. First of all, Jesus sends the Twelve out in pairs (Mark 6:7). We keep forgetting that we are being sent out two by two. We cannot bring the good news on our own. We are called to proclaim the gospel together, in community.[38]

Servant leaders must keep a balance between doing things themselves and encouraging others to participate. Although the leader may appear to have a team attitude, a person who does the team's work alone is not a genuine servant leader. Team ministry means going with others on mission to do what God has commissioned His leaders to do. Individualism is not a feature of servant leadership. Servant leaders empower members of the leadership team to achieve the shared goal. Warren Bennis explains why: "Basic changes take place very slowly, if at all, because those with the power generally have no knowledge, and those with the knowledge have no power."[39]

You can never go wrong following Jesus' example. He spent nearly three years with 12 of His closest followers, empowering them to carry out His mission in community after He ascended to the Father. Empowerment is both the spiritual leader's daily goal and method.

Chapter 20: *Radical Leader*

I t is easy for leaders to get so busy that they lose focus on mission. Granted, there is much to do: keeping up with email correspondence and voicemail messages, sitting in committee meetings, handling the latest crisis, meeting deadlines, writing performance evaluations; not to mention preparing meeting outlines, sermons and teaching outlines and newsletters. The central mission focus that was crystal clear in early ministry is now clouded by the pressing matters of the day. The important increasingly gives way to the urgent. Spiritual leaders must constantly remind themselves to "Keep the main thing, the main thing!"

Deliberate and intense focus on mission is a fundamental requisite for spiritual leadership. Like the apostle Paul, the leader must affirm, "I press on toward the goal to win the prize for which God has called me heavenward in Christ Jesus" (Philippians 3:14).

God does not call us to be obsessive, overzealous or counterproductive in our work. He summons us to be systematic, focused and radical in our dedication to His mission, the *Missio Dei,* fulfilling the Great Commission: "Therefore go and make disciples of all nations, baptizing them in the name of the Father and of the Son and of the Holy Spirit, and teaching them to obey everything I have commanded you. And surely I am with you always, to the very end of the age" (Matthew 28:19-20).

God calls spiritual leaders to be radicals, not fanatics. While the word "radical" has been corrupted by political realities of the times in which we live, the word itself is a strong, accurate description of the spiritual leader. Radical means "of, or pertaining to, the root." It evokes the leader who tenaciously focuses on a goal and moment by moment presses toward the fulfillment of that goal. Radical leadership begins with resolve and presses on to completion. Abraham Lincoln said it well: "Determine that the thing can and shall be done, and then we shall find a way."[40] Finding "the way" comes easier once the leader makes a radical commitment to the goal.

Few leaders better illustrate radical, determined leadership than William Booth, founder of The Salvation Army. In June 1904, the General was busier than ever as he prepared for the 15-day International Congress. Crowds would soon pack Royal Albert Hall, Exeter Hall, the Crystal Palace and the International Congress Hall. He had spent June 24 inspecting the congress sites. With only an hour to spare, he hastily prepared for an unexpected appointment. King Edward VII had summoned "the Rev. William Booth, Commander in Chief of The Salvation Army" to Buckingham Palace. With no time to spare, General Booth placed his top hat on a chair in the International Congress Hall, bent down and washed his hands in a workman's bucket. He was ready to meet the king. The audience with the king went well. Booth was delighted to speak of the Army's work in 49 countries. King Edward complimented him and asked how the churches viewed his work. "Sir," replied the 75-year-old General, "they imitate me."

The king was visibly amused by the General's reply and asked him to write in his autograph album. General Booth penned memorable words that encapsulate his life's focus on mission:

> *Some men's ambition is art.*
> *Some men's ambition is fame.*
> *Some men's ambition is gold.*
> *My ambition is the souls of men.*

The Founder was a radical spiritual leader; let us follow in his train.

Chapter 21: *Transformational Leader*

Nothing is permanent except change," said the Greek philosopher Heraclitus some 2,500 years ago. Change is an essential element of effective leadership. Leaders guide followers in changing the present and shaping the future. If nothing changes, the leader has failed. He or she has done little but follow the natural downward drift to complacency. The result of changeless leadership is a false, temporary sense of contentment. If nothing has changed, the status quo is preserved and progress dies.

Comic strips often provide truth and insight through humor. One *Calvin and Hobbes* tale begins with Calvin, the comic strip's *enfant terrible*, boasting, "I thrive on change." Hobbes, Calvin's lifelike stuffed tiger, responds, "You? You threw a fit this morning because your mother put less jelly on your toast than yesterday." What was Calvin's response? "I thrive on making *other* people change."

Human beings have twin primal urges. The first is to fear change for them, and the second is to want it for others. Leo Tolstoy observed, "Everybody thinks of changing humanity, and nobody thinks of changing himself."[41] For the spiritual leader, change must come from within. Mahatma Gandhi succinctly discerned, "You must be the change you wish to see in the world." Most people agree with the necessity of change, but very few people want to change. While change can be painful, it is often a prerequisite to survival and growth.

Change is a state of mind. Becoming an agent of change, a transformational spiritual leader, requires a sweeping evolution in attitude. A transformed leader is the requisite for a transformed Church. Transformation was at the heart of Paul's theology and ecclesiology. Paul challenged believers, especially spiritual leaders, to transform their attitudes. "Do not conform any longer to the pattern of this world," he pleaded, "but be transformed by the renewing of your mind. Then you will be able to test and approve what God's will is—His good, pleasing and perfect will" (Romans 12:2).

If you have tried to change an organizational structure, you have already met with resistance. You already know something about the difficulty in effecting change. You have experienced the strain and the enormous amount of time required to solve problems and persuade people to accept change. Resistance to change is a never-ending problem. The spiritual leader must remain steadfast in effecting change. Transformational leaders are agents of change. They become the difference between a revitalized and a deteriorating mission.

Noted theologian Reinhold Niebuhr wrote the Serenity Prayer. Millions have recited the prayer in Alcoholics Anonymous and other recovery programs around the world. It is also a prayer for the leader addicted to maintaining the status quo and not rocking the boat: "God give us grace to accept with serenity the things that cannot be changed, / the courage to change the things which should be changed, / and the wisdom to distinguish the one from the other."

In *Transformational Leadership,* Phillip Lewis reminds Christian leaders, "The future is now! And Christian leaders must be about the work of transforming themselves, others, and the Church. God is calling people to step into a new role: transformational leadership … His call is for a total revitalization and transformation of thinking and acting, for men and women to be leaders of change in His kingdom."[42] The good news is that it is never too late to become a transformational leader. All it takes is courage, strength and determination. In the words of George Eliot (Mary Ann Evans), "It is never too late to become what you might have been."

Chapter 22: *Decisive Leader*

No army ever claimed victory without decisive leadership. Decision-making is a fundamental responsibility of leadership. After careful analysis of circumstances and the considered input of colleagues, the leader must take action. Some decisions are uncomplicated and result in a positive outcome for everybody; these are the times when it is good to be the leader. However, rare are the moments when it is possible to make everybody happy. It is the hard decisions, the apparent no-win decisions, which cause frustration, agony and sleepless nights. In the words of Thomas Paine, "These are the times that try men's souls."[43] These are the times when the leader's decision—through the result of ardent prayer, meticulous analysis and full dialogue with colleagues and shared responsibility—causes pain and anguish for those negatively affected by the decision.

One of the hallmarks of poor leadership is the inability to make and follow through on difficult decisions. Decision and implementation are the dual responsibilities of efficient and effective spiritual leadership.

In the Old Testament, God made provision for the vital decision-making responsibilities of the high priest by giving explicit directions for the production of "the breastpiece of decision" as recorded in Exodus 28:29-30 (see also Leviticus 8:8):

> Whenever Aaron enters the Holy Place, he will bear the names of the sons of Israel over his heart on the breastpiece of decision as a continuing memorial before the Lord. Also put the Urim and the Thummim in the breastpiece, so they may be over Aaron's heart whenever he enters the presence of the Lord. Thus Aaron will always bear the means of making decisions for the Israelites over his heart before the Lord.

The nature of the *Urim* and the *Thummim* remains a mystery. The words do not have a literal meaning, although it is believed that *Thummim* is related to the Hebrew word *thom*, translated "integrity." The only certainty about the *Urim* and the *Thummim* is that they refer to some type of oracle device used by the high priest to determine God's will. They were used in conjunction with the "breastpiece of decision" that contained 12 gemstones representing the tribes of Israel. The *Urim* and the *Thummim* were likely two additional stones enclosed in a pouch placed inside the breastplate. These stones apparently gave the answers "yes" or "no" to questions put to them.

God provided direct, divine guidance to the high priest in the Old Covenant, and continues to do so in the New Covenant. Through Christ, Jeremiah's prophecy is fulfilled:

> **"The time is coming," declares the Lord, "when I will make a new covenant with the house of Israel … It will not be like the covenant I made with their forefathers … This is the covenant I will make with the house of Israel after that time … I will put my law in their minds and write it on their hearts. I will be their God, and they will be my people." (Jeremiah 31: 31-33)**

Spiritual leaders today must continue to make and implement decisions with a genuine, though invisible, divine "breastpiece of decision." They are obliged to "always bear the means of making decisions … over their hearts before the Lord" (Exodus 28:30). When a decision is made with integrity before God, the leader then must act. It is not the knowing but the doing of God's will that produces victory!

Chapter 23: *Creative Leader*

McNair Wilson, former Walt Disney Imagineer and founder of Imaginuity Unlimited, begins his popular seminars by asking the audience to make nine dots on a piece of paper as in the drawing below. He challenges everyone to connect all nine dots without removing the pen from the paper, using only four straight lines. Before reading further, try it. If you solve the puzzle within 10 minutes, you need not read the remainder of this chapter. You will have visually mastered this axiom of leadership. (Answer at the end of this chapter, but don't look now!)

```
•        •        •

•        •        •

•        •        •
```

In order to solve the puzzle you must first reject the assumption that you are required to draw within the box. The solution is only achieved by drawing lines that extend outside the box.

A leader solves problems. Solving organizational and relational challenges often requires the spiritual leader to think, plan and act "outside the box." Effective leaders think creatively—beyond the usual way of looking at a situation.

In *The 7 Habits of Highly Effective People,* Stephen Covey admits that the creative process is the most terrifying part of leadership because the leader does not know exactly what is going to happen or where it is going to lead. "Without doubt," Covey warns, "you have to leave the comfort zone of base camp and confront an entirely new and unknown wilderness. You become a trailblazer, a pathfinder. You open new possibilities, new territories, new continents, so that others can follow."[44] Biblical leaders were often forced to think, plan and act in innovative ways. For stubborn, traditional leaders like Elijah, thinking and acting in new ways was difficult. Instead of rejoicing after the miraculous defeat of the 450 prophets of Baal and 400 prophets of Asherah on Mt. Carmel (1 Kings 18), Elijah panicked. Upon receiving Queen Jezebel's threatening message, he ran in terror. "May the gods deal with me," she warned, "be it ever so severely, if by this time tomorrow I do not make your life like that of one of them" (1 Kings 19:2). The prophetic champion of Mt. Carmel fled in defeat to Mt. Horeb, "the mountain of God," where he hid in a cave.

The Lord ordered him to "stand on the mountain in the presence of the Lord," for He was about to instruct the prophet in a better way: "Then a great and powerful wind tore the mountains apart and shattered the rocks before the Lord, but the Lord was not in the wind. After the wind there was an earthquake, but the Lord was not in the earthquake. After the earthquake came a fire, but the Lord was not in the fire. And after the fire came a gentle whisper" (1 Kings 19:11-12). The controlling, powerful elements of wind, earthquake and fire were the customary ways of handling challenges in the ancient world. But God wanted Elijah to try a different approach, one that came in an unusual way—a divine whisper. God whispered an "out of the box" solution, as recorded in 1 Kings 19:15-18. When you face a challenging situation, a perplexing set of circumstances, a tough decision, try the gentle whisper approach. *Listen* to God's whisper deep in your heart; *pray*, seek a new approach; *act*, do something new.

An old chorus reminds leaders of the secret to new adventures in faith:

> *Faith, mighty faith,*
> *The promise sees,*
> *And looks to that above.*
> *Laughs at impossibilities,*
> *And cries, "It shall be done!"*

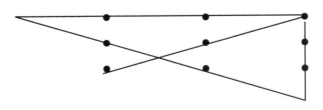

Chapter 24: *Look Both Ways*

The Romans pictured Janus, god of beginnings and transitions, with two faces, one on either side of his head. Janus could look forward and backward simultaneously. As the fabled custodian of the universe, Janus served as the perpetual guardian of gates and doors. The first hour of the day, the first day of the month and the first month of the year were sacred to Janus. January bears his name because it is the month of transition, the gateway from the old year to the new. The word "janitor" comes from Janus, since he was the guardian of what janitors clean and care for: gates, doors and passageways.

While Janus is but a mythological deity, he is known today for a leadership principle. The Janusian principle recognizes that beginnings must be approached by looking forward and backward at the same time. More than ever before, the Church and the world needs leaders who carefully study the past while planning the future—leaders with a bold understanding of history and mission. The writers of the New Testament preserved this principle through the use of a unique Greek verb construction known as the perfect tense. This tense depicts a completed action that has lingering effects or that leaves an ongoing result or condition. Speakers of modern languages do not have the capability of communicating in the past and present tenses at the same time. The thought "and now still is" aptly recaptures the meaning of the perfect tense when supplied in translation. For example, Hebrews 2:9 can accurately be translated, "But we see Jesus … crowned [and now still is crowned] with glory and honor … " Another example is Hebrews 12:2, "Jesus … who for the joy set before Him endured the cross … and sat down [and now still is seated] at the right hand of the throne of God."

The sense most often conveyed by the perfect tense, however, is the continuing *effect* of the action (not the action itself), which must be determined in each context. For example, in Jesus' cry from the cross, "It is finished [and now continues the result of this apparent ending]!" (John 19:30), the perfect tense reveals that the effects of His sacrificial death are anything but finished. Another instance in which a particular action is finished but the effects have a profoundly important ongoing significance is in Galatians 2:20—"I have been [and now still am] crucified with Christ" The past action looks ahead to present and future reality.

Few abilities are more essential to effective leadership than the ability to simultaneously look backward and forward, recognizing the connection between the past and present. Spiritual leadership requires a discerning knowledge of the past, a realistic understanding of the present and a clear vision for the future. As Sydney J. Harris, reporter for the *Chicago Sun-Times,* pointed out, "People are fond of saying that 'the past is dead,' but actually it is the future that is dead—and we make it come alive only by applying what we have learned from the living past to the present."

The Salvation Army's 10th General, Clarence Wiseman, has noted: "When the dilemmas of history are held up to the light by those who stand humbly in the presence of the Creator, their place in the ultimate scheme of things gradually becomes clearer. Not only is it true that 'the Lord God omnipotent reigneth,' but it is equally true that God will vindicate His promise in the book of Revelation, 'Behold, I am making all things new.'"[45]

Chapter 25: *Transition Well*

The most important factor in a relay race is the baton pass from one runner to the next. The race can be won or lost in the split second it takes for the baton to change hands. Synchronization of the runners' pace, timing and placement of the baton, grip and acceleration—every tiny aspect of the hand-off—plays an essential role in this decisive moment. As the fresh runner receives the baton, an apprehensive hush comes over the spectators. In this heart-stopping moment, both runners and onlookers experience overwhelming emotions of celebration and anticipation. A successful hand-off celebrates the runner who has finished well, and at the same time anticipates the next sprinter's winning lap.

Likewise, the passing of the baton of spiritual leadership is a crucial time for God's people. A smooth transition from one leader to another sets the pace for future advances. In the race to fulfill the Great Commission (Matthew 28:18-20), leadership change is normal, healthy and essential. It affords a divine moment for fervent celebration and confident anticipation.

Nearing the end of his life's journey, Paul sent Timothy what would be the apostle's final epistle. In the final chapter, he celebrates his courageous earthly race. "I have fought the good fight," he testifies. "I have finished the race, I have kept the faith. Now there is in store for me the crown of righteousness, which the Lord, the righteous Judge, will award to me on that day—and not only to me, but also to all who have longed for his appearing" (2 Timothy 4:7-8). The Lord expects His appointed spiritual leaders to celebrate the race's finish. Paul graphically describes the victory celebration as belonging to every faithful disciple who completes his or her stretch of the race: "But thanks be to God, who always leads us in triumphal procession in Christ and through us spreads everywhere the fragrance of the knowledge of Him" (2 Corinthians 2:14). For God's people, transition must be a time of joyful, triumphant procession.

After the hand-off, the focus shifts to the new runner. For followers of Christ, the best days are always ahead. The cycle of celebration and anticipation continues throughout this temporal race—a race that will only finish with the Lord's glorious return. His appearance will signal the end of the race. In the meantime, one thing is certain, the Lord will not leave His Bride, the Church, without His appointed and anointed leaders. "You did not choose Me," Jesus reminded His disciples, "but I chose you and appointed you to go and bear fruit—fruit that will last. Then the Father will give you whatever you ask in My name" (John 15:16).

Jesus carefully chose those who would lead His Church. Luke 6:12-19 records the events surrounding the choosing of the twelve disciples:

> **Jesus went out to a mountainside to pray, and spent the night praying to God. When morning came, He called His disciples to Him and chose twelve of them, whom He also designated apostles … He went down with them … A large crowd of His disciples was there and a great number of people … who had come to hear Him and to be healed of their diseases.**

What was Jesus praying about before He called and commissioned His disciples? The answer is found in verse 13: "When the morning came, He called His disciples to Him and chose twelve of them." He spent all night praying about to whom He would pass the baton.

Jesus set the example for discerning God's will in appointing spiritual leaders. One should pray earnestly for guidance, make a decision and work hand in hand with the newly appointed leaders in the splendid adventure of building the Kingdom.

Chapter 26: *Weigh Criticism*

What a foolish idea! It will never work! The plan is bound to fail! Are you serious?" Rare is the spiritual leader who does not routinely hear these and similar criticisms of ideas or actions. While often well intended, such negative voices cruelly discourage creativity.

The existence of critics is inevitable. Benjamin Franklin commented, "In this world nothing is certain but death and taxes."[46] He was wrong. Criticism is the third certainty of life. If you are alive, you have at least one critic. As Elbert Hubbard reportedly said, "To avoid criticism, do nothing, say nothing, and be nothing."

The Author of creativity, on the other hand, wants His people to take risks in fulfilling the Great Commission. He wants His spiritual leaders to put feet in their faith. God is unable to effectively use leaders whose main concern is "What will the neighbors think?" or "What do the opinion polls reveal?" Spiritual leaders must be willing to sacrifice and take risks with their public image.

After many years in business, Laurie Beth Jones concluded that Jesus' leadership approach with His staff ran counter to most of the management styles and techniques employed today. This is especially true in the area of public image. In *Jesus, CEO*, Jones asks, "What do each of these characters have in common?"[47]

- A deluded engineer
- A magician
- A waiter
- A nudist
- A beggar

- A lunatic
- A harem girl
- An improper woman
- A blasphemer

They were assumed or assigned to the following:

- Noah (designed and built the ark in the middle of a desert)
- Moses (turned water into blood)
- Nehemiah (was cupbearer to a king)
- Isaiah (went naked for three years)
- Elijah (had to ask a widow for food)
- King David (acted insane to escape his captors)
- Queen Esther (made her way to the top of the king's list)
- Mary (conceived a child before marriage)
- Jesus (claimed to be equal with God)

Each of these biblical characters assumed roles that were misunderstood by their critics. Their public image was shattered. Despite the anticipated consequences of their words and actions, they were prepared to risk position and reputation to fulfill God's plan.

Jesus was willing to look foolish. His detractors criticized Him for riding into Jerusalem on a donkey, for befriending sinners, for failing to bring enough wine to the wedding reception. His words and actions never failed to draw heated criticism.

Spiritual leaders take risks and refuse to be discouraged by detractors. Before Nobel Prize winners like Guglielmo Marconi invented wireless telegraphy and Pierre and Marie Curie discovered radium, their fellow scientists ridiculed them. Critics laughed at Thomas Edison's many failures until one incandescent bulb glowed.

In fairness, it is important to note that critics play an indispensable role in challenging leaders to greatness. E. Stanley Jones called critics "the unpaid guardians of my soul." With the writer of Proverbs, Dr. Jones understood that his critics kept him humble and focused, "Like an earring of gold or an ornament of fine gold is a wise man's rebuke to a listening ear" (Proverbs 25:12).

How much should leaders listen to their critics? Harry Ironside gives wise counsel: "If what they are saying about you is true, mend your ways. If it is not true, forget it, and go on and serve the Lord."

As always, Jesus has the good word, the benediction, on criticism. If you are being criticized (and we all raise our hands), Jesus reminds us all that "Blessed are you when people insult you, persecute you and falsely say all kinds of evil against you because of Me. Rejoice and be glad, because great is your reward in heaven, for in the same way they persecuted the prophets who were before you" (Matthew 5:11-12).

Chapter 27: *Accept Loneliness*

Three Dog Night, a rock band in the late 1960s, had a signature song that reminded that generation of a poignant fact of life. The popular song lamented the loneliness of a solitary life: "One is the loneliest number that you'll ever do. / One is the loneliest number."

The spiritual leader's position is often lonely. In the end, he or she must make final decisions alone. Family, friends and associates may provide input and recommend action, but the leader alone must decide. In the words of Max Lucado, "A man who wants to lead the orchestra must turn his back on the crowd."

Commissioner Bramwell Tripp of The Salvation Army offered helpful commentary to a young officer on the loneliness of leadership. "The more encompassing the leader's responsibility," he noted, "the fewer true friends he or she will enjoy. The spiritual leader has a kinship with the lonely long distance runner. He or she often runs alone."

In *Mastering the Old Testament,* John Maxwell observes: "Perhaps the most sobering fact of leadership is that it is a lonely position. A leader has no one with whom he shares the responsibility of final decisions. It is human to stand with the crowd; it is divine to stand alone. It is manlike to follow the people, to drift with the tide; it is Godlike to follow a principle and stem the tide."[48] The Bible abounds with illustrations of leaders who had to stand alone. Noah built an ark and sailed the seas with only his family for support. His neighbors laughed at his peculiarity, and they perished. Abraham wandered the wilderness and worshiped alone on Mt. Moriah. The citizens of Sodom laughed at the eccentric shepherd, turned their back on Lot and fed the flames of God's wrath. Daniel dined and prayed alone in Babylon. Elijah sacrificed and witnessed alone. Jeremiah prophesied and wept alone. Jesus loved and died alone. In Paul's final epistle to his young protégé, Timothy, the weary, battle-scarred apostle remembered his appearance before the emperor and lamented, "At my first defense, no one came to my support, but everyone deserted me" (2 Timothy 4:16).

As Jesus walked with His disciples from the upper room to the Garden of Gethsemane only 12 hours before His crucifixion, He warned them about the persecution to come. He told them where, when and why He was going, and finally assured them that when they felt abandoned, they would not be alone. He would send "another Counselor," the Holy Spirit (John 14:16), who would never forsake them. Jesus knew what lay ahead, and He did not want the disciples' faith shaken or destroyed. His promise to them remains His promise to twenty-first-century disciples: "when He, the Spirit of truth, comes, He will guide you into all truth. He will not speak on his own; He will speak only what he hears, and He will tell you what is yet to come. He will bring glory to Me by taking from what is Mine and making it known to you" (John 16:13-14).

God wants you, His chosen spiritual leader, to realize that you are never alone. You have the Holy Spirit to comfort you, to give you strength and courage, to teach you truth, and help you in all circumstances. Listen anew to His final words of command and comfort before ascending to His Father: "Therefore go and make disciples of all nations, baptizing them in the name of the Father and of the Son and of the Holy Spirit, and teaching them to obey everything I have commanded you. And surely I am with you always, to the very end of the age" (Matthew 28:19-20).

Chapter 28: *Be Positive*

B ing Crosby was right. In his 1945 World War II movie, *Here Come the Waves,* he looked into Betty Hutton's eyes and crooned an indispensable tenet of leadership: "You've got to accentuate the positive, / Eliminate the negative, / And latch on to the affirmative / Don't mess with Mister In-between." This could be a leadership theme song.

Spiritual leadership is often discussed in positive terms. After all, it is a high and positive calling. However, it is also helpful to reflect on the negative side of leadership in order to more fully appreciate the positive. The New Testament character Diotrephes, whose name means, "nourished by Jupiter," was an unfit leader whose pride and self-exultation resulted in a spirit of elitism and stubbornness. Diotrephes latched on to the negatives of leadership. The apostle John exposes him and the negative effects of his leadership in 3 John 9-11:

> I wrote to the church, but Diotrephes, who loves to be first, will have nothing to do with us. So if I come, I will call attention to what he is doing, gossiping maliciously about us. Not satisfied with that, he refuses to welcome the brothers. He also stops those who want to do so and puts them out of the church. Dear friend, do not imitate what is evil but what is good. Anyone who does what is good is from God. Anyone who does what is evil has not seen God.

Through his description of Diotrephes, John describes negative characteristics that render an individual unfit for effective, spiritual leadership. An unfit leader: seeks to be first and to be noticed; refuses to submit to spiritual authority; gossips and enjoys defaming others; controls others; and drives away those who will not submit to his or her authority

The Lord has no patience with leaders who are "false shepherds." Ezekiel records a harsh warning to leaders who neglect and exploit those for whom they are responsible. "As surely as I live," declares the Sovereign Lord, "because My flock lacks a shepherd and so has been plundered and has become food for all the wild animals, and because My shepherds did not search for My flock but cared for themselves rather than for My flock, therefore ... I am against the shepherds and will hold them accountable for My flock" (Ezekiel 34:8-10).

The New Testament also carries warnings against self-centered, negative leaders. Jesus declared, "The hired hand is not the shepherd who owns the sheep. So when he sees the wolf coming, he abandons the sheep and runs away. Then the wolf attacks the flock and scatters it. The man runs away because he is a hired hand and cares nothing for the sheep" (John 10:12-13).

In his farewell address to the leaders of the Church in Ephesus, Paul cautions them to watch out for unfit leaders. "I know that after I leave," says the apostle, "savage wolves will come in among you and will not spare the flock. Even from your own number men will arise and distort the truth in order to draw away disciples after them. So be on your guard!" (Acts 20:29-31). These false leaders, warns Paul, are those who "preach Christ out of selfish ambition, not sincerely" (Philip 1:17). Leaders have a choice. They can cling to their conferred, temporary authority for selfish ends, or they can use their influence to guide and nurture those who look to them for direction. Jesus' call to His spiritual leaders is a call to the positive. His is a call to a life of sacrificial service, a call to accentuate the positive and eliminate the negative; "don't mess with Mr. In-between!"

Chapter 29: *Solve Problems*

L eaders solve problems. The first step in solving a problem is to change its description. Reclassify problems as challenges. Effective leaders adjust their vocabulary, eliminating the word "problem," along with "impossible," "never," "hopeless" and related negative words and expressions.

The spiritual leader "laughs at impossibilities, and cries it shall be done!" Without God, "laughing at impossibilities" is naïve at best and foolhardy at worst. God alone transforms impossibilities into accomplishments. When the disciples were discouraged by the lesson taught in the parable of the rich young ruler, Jesus reminded them that, "With man this is impossible, but with God all things are possible" (Matthew 19:26). Spiritual leaders tenaciously embrace an "all things are possible" attitude.

The leader's objective in facing a challenge is to determine and implement the best solution. This process has three tiers.

The leader's first responsibility is to *define reality.* The most brilliant, creative plan will fail if it is based on misinformation, half-truths or romanticized idealism. A newly promoted leader received an unexpected comment from a well-wisher, who prophesied, "You have heard the truth for the last time!" This must not happen. The spiritual leader is obliged to find, understand and accept the reality of all the challenges that are faced.

Acts 15 recounts the first council of the first-century Church. The leaders met in Jerusalem to solve the controversy over whether a Gentile must first follow Jewish law in order to become a Christian. "The apostles and elders met to consider this question," Luke records. "After much discussion, Peter got up and addressed them." After Peter defined reality, the crisis was further considered, as "the whole assembly became silent as they listened to Barnabas and Paul telling about the miraculous signs and wonders God had done among the Gentiles through them" (Acts 15:6-12).

Once reality is defined and understood, the next step is to *determine the goal*. A clear definition of the objective is vital to the success of any project. After defining and illustrating the dilemma faced by the early Church, James stated the goal. "Brothers, listen to me. Simon has described to us how God at first showed his concern by taking from the Gentiles a people for himself … It is my judgment, therefore, that we should not make it difficult for the Gentiles who are turning to God" (Acts 15:13-19). James clearly articulated the objective—they must find a way to allow Gentiles easy access to the grace of the Lord without requiring that they first become Jewish.

The final step is to *design and activate*. Designing and activating a solution to a perplexing challenge often requires a paradigm shift, sometimes referred to as "thinking outside the box." The word "paradigm" comes from Greek. Originally a scientific term, it is commonly used today to mean a model, theory or assumption. Thomas Kuhn introduced the term "paradigm shift" in his influential book *The Structure of Scientific Revolutions*. Kuhn demonstrated that nearly every significant scientific breakthrough started with a break with tradition and with old ways of thinking.

Outside the scientific world, we can think of a paradigm shift as a change from one way of thinking to another. It is not just something that is new and innovative, it is revolutionary, transformational. It is a type of metamorphosis. Paradigm shifts do not just happen, but rather agents of change drive them. The spiritual leader, while holding on to the essence of past values, does not fear changing the form in order to better meet the goal. Essence must never change, but form must always be open to change.

After accepting the goal stated by James, the Jerusalem Council designed a solution as recorded in Acts 15:20-35. Paul and his colleagues would take a letter to the Gentiles in Antioch explaining the official policy now agreed on by the fledgling Church—a revolutionary, transformational policy that was the Church's first major paradigm shift. For the first time, Gentile believers were not first required to become Jewish proselytes before becoming Christians.

"Can do" leadership is achieved first by clearly defining reality, then by determining the goal. The final step of designing a solution is the most challenging and may require a revolutionary, transformational paradigm shift. With the apostle Paul, the Lord's twenty-first-century spiritual leaders must face every leadership challenge with the determined affirmation, "I can do everything through Him who gives me strength" (Philippians 4:13).

Chapter 30: *Cultivate Good Habits*

I n *The 7 Habits of Highly Effective People*, Stephen Covey develops the leadership paradigm he identifies as "inside-out leadership." He bases the seven habits of effective leadership on the idea that, while we cannot change all situations, we can and must first change ourselves from the inside out.

A quarter century after its publication, Covey's book remains a bestseller. Every spiritual leader should read this classic. While widely applauded in the secular world, the book is based on solid biblical principles. Before detailing his seven habits, Covey quotes Ezra Taft Benson's discerning words on a leader's foundational need for inner spiritual training: "The Lord works from the inside out. The world works from the outside in. The world would take people out of the slums. Christ takes the slums out of people, and then they take themselves out of the slums ... The world would shape human behavior, but Christ can change human behavior."

Covey's book has exceptional advice on leadership, life management and relationships, all founded on the inside-out biblical concept. Behavior, Covey contends, is learned, not instinctive. The good news is that you can discard old habits and replace them with new, more effective habits. Every spiritual leader should memorize and endeavor to emulate the following seven leadership habits. Transforming each declaration into a personal habit will revolutionize the spiritual leader and the effectiveness that results.

Habit 1: Be Proactive (Initiate) – Effective people truly lead their lives. Instead of saying, "It's hopeless," they say, "Let's look at the alternatives." Instead of yearning, "If only," they affirm, "I will."

Habit 2: Begin with the End in Mind (Creativity) – In all successful endeavors, the initial creation is mental or spiritual, and the second is physical. Effective leaders envision what they want and how to get it. They habitually pick priorities stemming from their basic values.

Habit 3: Put First Things First (Productivity) – Putting first things first is at the heart of effective leadership. It requires wise management, using our four human endowments of self-awareness, imagination, conscience and will to accomplish the most important things.

Habit 4: Think Win-Win (Interdependence) – Win-win thinking is a frame of mind that seeks mutual benefit in all human interaction. This endeavor seeks agreements and solutions that are satisfying to all involved.

Habit 5: Seek First to Understand, then to be Understood (Empathy) – Leaders must be careful not to prescribe before they diagnose. Spiritual leaders have a tendency to rush in, attempting to fix things up with "good advice," but without reflective understanding.

Habit 6: Synergize (Valuing Differences) – "Synergy" implies that the whole is greater than the sum of its parts. Synergistic communication begins with the assumption that cooperating individuals will share insights and open their minds and hearts. The spiritual leader values the differences among team members and seeks to engender unity through diversity.

Habit 7: Sharpen the Saw (Consistency) – Sharpening the saw entails preserving, renewing and enhancing the greatest asset in every leader's possession, the self. The leader's daily goal must be to continually formulate a personal program that balances the four dimensions of human nature: physical, spiritual, mental and emotional health.

Effective spiritual leadership must involve forming good habits. As Ralph Waldo Emerson aptly said, "That which we persist in doing becomes easier—not that the nature of the task has changed, but our ability to do has increased." Habits centered on accurate, biblical leadership principles will increase the spiritual leader's ability to live a peaceful, harmonized, loving and effective life while engaged in the awesome task of fulfilling the Great Commission (Matthew 28:18-20).

Chapter 31: *Develop Winning Strategies*

S piritual leaders are called to serve an ailing world, to offer hope in seemingly hopeless situations. The task is enormous, and the results are often discouraging. The apostle Paul makes clear what causes periodic discouragement: "For our struggle is not against flesh and blood, but against the rulers, against the authorities, against the powers of this dark world and against the spiritual forces of evil in the heavenly realms" (Ephesians 6:12).

The answer to successfully confronting overwhelming and discouraging circumstances may be found in three winning strategies:

The first strategy is discipline. In the first chapter of Proverbs, Solomon declares that God offers wisdom to leaders who seek it through ardent prayer and passionate discipline. The first seven verses of chapter one sum up the purpose and theme for his proverbs: "The proverbs of Solomon … for gaining wisdom and instruction; for understanding words of insight; for receiving instruction in prudent behavior, doing what is right and just and fair" (Proverbs 1:1-4). Solomon concludes his prologue with the theme verse for all of the Proverbs that follow: "The fear of the Lord is the beginning of knowledge, but fools despise wisdom and discipline" (Proverbs 1:7). Discipline is the prerequisite for effective leadership. Successful leadership begins and ends with a disciplined life.

The second strategy is visibility. Spiritual leaders are called to be visible beacons of light in a dark and gloomy world. Jesus commands, "Let your light shine before men, that they may see your good deeds and praise your Father in heaven" (Matthew 5:16). Spiritual leaders must perpetually let their light shine.

We live in an age when it is fashionable for leaders to spend more time in their offices than with their people. Actually meeting with and talking to people is a time-consuming and messy journey. However, the answers to the challenging problems of life take time, dialogue and human contact.

The final winning strategy is devotion. Jesus said, "No one can serve two masters. Either he will hate the one and love the other, or he will be devoted to the one and despise the other. You cannot serve both God and money" (Matthew 6:24). The Greek word for "devotion" is *eulabes*. It means addicted, loyal, faithful, devout, dutiful and established. *Eulabes* is generally translated as "devout" or "godly." Spiritual leaders are men and women who are addicted to God. It is the only addiction that will lead to triumph, not trouble.

The only adequate solution to the perplexing, complicated, fragile ministry to which the spiritual leader has been called—the only means of victory—is to be utterly devoted to God. Begin and end each day with intimate communion with Him.

For the spiritual leader these three strategies remain: discipline, visibility and devotion. Live by these and God will accomplish His transforming work through you.

Chapter 32: *Follow the Fundamentals*

Christopher Liebenberg, chairman of the board for NED Bank in South Africa and former chairman of The Salvation Army Advisory Board in Johannesburg, identifies four fundamentals of leadership: create a vision, set some goals, get the right person into the job and go play golf (or substitute your favorite pastime). Liebenberg's leadership essentials provide our outline for leadership's foundational principles.

First, create a vision. Vision is a requisite for spiritual leadership. Leaders envision the future and challenge the impossible. They see deeper and further than others. Illustrious agents of change such as Gandhi, Churchill, Meir, Sadat, Mandela and King were leaders who accomplished what others considered impossible.

Next, set goals. Setting goals and expectations is the essential next step to fulfilling a vision. Goals and objectives are the stepping-stones to realizing the vision. Stephen Covey observes:

> The cause of almost all relationship difficulties is rooted in conflicting or ambiguous expectations around roles and goals. Whether we are dealing with the question of who does what at work, how you communicate with your daughter when you tell her to clean her room, or who feeds the fish and takes out the garbage, we can be certain that unclear expectations will lead to misunderstanding, disappointment, and withdrawals of trust.[49]

Liebenberg's third principle is arguably the most crucial. Leaders cannot achieve the clearest defined goal, let alone the ultimate vision, without the help of others. Leadership is not singular. The beginning and end of servant leadership is community. Leaders both serve the community and depend on the community to lead. In the words of Luciano De Crescenzo,

"We are all angels with only one wing; we can only fly while embracing one another." It takes a team to realize a vision. Once the right person is found, the leader must set that individual free to accomplish the agreed-upon goals. Some supervision is required, but obsessive accountability is counterproductive.

Finally, go and play. While the first three steps are accepted leadership principles, the fourth may sound lighthearted, even flippant. Liebenberg's concluding principle is, however, as important as the first three. Unless the spiritual leader finds time to refresh, reflect and refocus, the first three steps will become increasingly difficult.

From the beginning of Creation, God provided for a day of rest, reflection and renewal. Jesus instructed the questioning Pharisees by reminding them that "the Sabbath was made for man, not man for the Sabbath" (Mark 2:27). God requires His leaders to take a regular break from the challenges of administration. Rest is a divine imperative, not an option.

Jesus often sought solitude in the hills of Galilee to renew Himself. Spiritual leaders must follow the Master's example. The leader's ultimate recreation comes from the assurance of God's abiding presence. "He who dwells in the shelter of the Most High will rest in the shadow of the Almighty" (Psalm 91:1). Relax; God is in control.

God's chosen spiritual leader should begin each day with prayer. I recommend that the prayer's concluding refrain be: "Lord, with the mind of Christ and power of the Holy Spirit, guide and empower me today to create a vision, set some goals, get the right person and go have fun."

PART II: ADVICE FOR LEADERS

Chapter 33: *Never Give Up*

It was surprisingly painless to pick the theme for this final chapter. The topic came to mind immediately. The focus highlights the underpinning universal and foundational quality for spiritual leadership, the consistent quality that marks all successful leaders: perseverance.

Winston Churchill visited the Harrow School on October 29, 1941. He had come to hear the traditional songs he had sung there as a youth and to speak to the students. His brief address became one of his most quoted. Churchill concluded by reiterating the indispensable characteristic of leadership. "Never, ever, ever, ever, ever, ever, ever, give up. Never give up. Never give up. Never give up."

Church history overflows with examples of leaders who never gave up. William Carey (1761-1834) was a Baptist pastor who sensed God's call to India. His distinguished 41-year missionary service in India got off to a shaky start when his passage ended up in the hands of the wrong shipping agent. Upon his eventual arrival in India, Carey was not permitted into the country, so he was forced to take refuge in the Danish colony at Serampore. After years of translating the Bible into one of the Indian languages, he found that his assistant was leading him astray in the linguistic interpretation of the biblical words. When Carey and his fellow workers had eventually completed the manuscripts of several Indian languages, they stored the only copies in a building. One night, the building caught fire and all the manuscripts were destroyed. But William Carey never gave up! Because of his perseverance, when he died at 73, he was responsible for having the Scriptures translated and printed into forty languages. In addition, Carey had been a college professor and founded a college at Serampore. He witnessed India opening its doors to missionaries—all this because he never gave up.

General John Larsson, past international leader of The Salvation Army, conferred on Commissioner Harry Williams the Order of the Founder, The Salvation Army's highest award, at a ceremony at International Headquarters in 2005. At 92, Commissioner Williams was a living example of never giving up. For 30 years he served with this wife, Eileen, in four of the Army's major hospitals on the Indian subcontinent. He became an authority on plastic surgery. In 2005, he was admitted to the Order of the British Empire.

Following the presentation ceremony, the ever-energetic Williams breezed through a brief history of his globetrotting ministry. He testified that his experiences confirmed the power of God to bring victory from the ashes of apparent defeat, as long as he never gave up. Whether stomping countless miles in the Himalayas, or laden with medicines in the Andes of Bolivia, or on daring flights during his work at a makeshift hospital in Saigon during the Vietnam War or on his way to remote parts of Papua New Guinea by helicopter, Commissioner Harry Williams always embodied his life's creed, "Never give up!"

The writer of Hebrews summarizes the foundation of spiritual leadership by challenging Christians to follow the example of those in the past for whom their life motto remained staying the course. The writer concludes, "Since we are surrounded by such a great cloud of witnesses, let us throw off everything that hinders and the sin that so easily entangles, and let us run with perseverance the race marked out for us" (Hebrews 12:1).

Supporting all the qualities of spiritual leaders is the tenacity of character and purpose, which boldly affirms, even in the most difficult of circumstances, "With God's grace and strength, I will never, ever, ever, ever, ever, ever, ever, give up!"

Notes

1 Henri J.M. Nouwen, *In the Name of Jesus: Reflections on Christian Leadership* (New York: Crossroads Publishing, 1991) 31-32

2 *Ibid*, 73

3 Samuel L. Brengle, *The Soul-Winner's Secret* (London: Salvationist Publishing and Supplies, 1960) 22-23

4 Leith Anderson, *A Church for the 21st Century* (Minneapolis: Bethany, 1992) 222

5 Douglas K. Smith, "The Following Part of Leading" in *The Leader of the Future,* ed. by Frances Hesselbein, Marshall Goldsmith, and Richard Beckhard (San Francisco: Jossey-Bass, 1997) 199-200

6 J. Oswald Sanders, *Spiritual Leadership* (Chicago: Moody Press, 1967) 105

7 C. Gene Wilkes, *Jesus on Leadership* (Wheaton, IL: Tyndale House Publishers, 1998) 73

8 C.W. Hall, *Samuel Logan Brengle* (New York: The Salvation Army, 1933) 271

9 J. Oswald Sanders, *Spiritual Leadership* (Chicago: Moody Press, 2007) 25

10 Nouwen, 62

11 Malcolm Muggeridge, *A Twentieth Century Testimony* (Nashville: Thomas Nelson, 1978) 72

12 T.E. Lawrence, *Seven Pillars of Wisdom: a Triumph* (London: Privately Published, 1922)

13 Powhatan W. James, *George W. Truett: a Biography* (Literary Licensing, LLC, 2011)

14 William Booth, *Seven Spirits; or What I Teach My Officers* (London: Simpkin, Marshall, Hamilton, Kent & Co., Ltd., 1907) 105

15 Lovett Weems, Jr., *Leadership in the Wesleyan Spirit* (Nashville: Abingdon Press, 1999) 135

16 Lytton Strachey, *Eminent Victorians: Cardinal Manning, Dr. Arnold, Florence Nightingale and General Gordon* (New York: The Modern Library, 1918) 151

17 Max DePree, *Leadership is an Art* (New York: Random House LLC, 2011) 11

18 William Law, *A Serious Call to a Devout and Holy Life – the Spirit of Love* (New York: Paulist Press, 1978) 259

19 Peter Drucker, *Managing for the Future* (New York: Routledge Press, 2011) 103

20 Samuel Logan Brengle, *Ancient Prophets and Modern Problems* (Atlanta: The Salvation Army, 1978)

21 C.H. Spurgeon, *Spurgeon's Devotional Bible* (Darlington: Evangelical Press, 1996) 749

22 Donald E. Demaray, *Laughter Joy and Healing* (Grand Rapids, MI: Baker Book House, 1986) 13

23 A. E. Norrish, *Christian Leadership* (Delhi, India: Masihi Sahitya Sanstha, 1965) 28

24 Helmut Thielicke, *Encounter with Spurgeon* (Cambridge, UK: James Clarke Lutterworth, 1964) 26

25 J. Oswald Sanders, *Spiritual Leadership – A Commitment to Excellence for Every Believer* (Chicago: Moody Publishers, 2007)

26 Thielicke, 14

27 Gallup, Inc., Poll taken Dec. 5-8, 2013

28 D.T. Phillips, *Lincoln on Leadership—Executive Strategies for Tough Times* (New York: Warner Books, 1992) 56-57

29 Stephen R. Covey, *The 7 Habits of Highly Effective People* (New York: Simon & Schuster, 1989) 148

30 J. Oswald Sanders, 44-45

31 J.R. Andrews, *George Whitefield, a Light Rising in Obscurity* (London: Morgan and Scott, 1915) 410-11

32 James M. Kouzes and Barry Z. Posner, *The Leadership Challenge* (New York: Warner Books, 1994) 8

33 Joel Arthur Barker, *Future Edge* (New York: William Morrow, 1992) 71

34 Doug Murren, *Leadership* (Ventura, CA: Regal, 1994) 128

35 Phillip V. Lewis, *Transformational Leadership—A New Model for Total Church Involvement* (Nashville, Tennessee: Broadman & Holman, 1996) 85

36 K.G. Prunty, "Jesus: The Inner Side of Leadership," in K.F. Hall, ed., *Living Leadership: Biblical Leadership Speaks to Our Day* (Anderson, IN: Scripture Press, 1991) 161

37 Paul Hersey, *The Situational Leader* (Escondido, CA: Center for Leadership Studies, 1997) 48-51

38 Nouwen, 40

39 Warren Bennis, *Why Leaders Can't Lead* (San Francisco: Jossey-Bass, 1989) 30

40 Gordon Leidner, *Abraham Lincoln: Quotes, Quips and Speeches,* (Naperville, IL, Sourcebooks, Inc., 2009)

[41] Leo Tolstoy, *Some Social Remedies*, Pamphlets Translated from Russian (Christchurch Hants, England: The Free Age Press, 1900) 71

[42] Lewis, 1

[43] Thomas Paine, *The American Crisis*, vol. 1 Dec. 1779, a series of 13 articles written between 1776 and 1783, (Personal Essay, 1779), 1

[44] Covey, 263

[45] Clarence Wiseman, *A Burning in My Bones* (Toronto: McGraw-Hill Ryerson Ltd., 1979)

[46] Benjamin Franklin, "To Jean Baptiste Le Roy November 13 1789" in Albert Henry Smyth ed., *The Writings of Benjamin Franklin, Volume 10,* (Macmillan, 1907)

[47] Laurie Beth Jones, *Jesus, CEO* (New York: Hyperion, 1995) 43-44

[48] John Maxwell, *Mastering the Old Testament Commentary,* Vol. 5 (Word Publishing, 1987) 329

[49] Covey, 194

CREST BOOKS

Salvation Army National Publications

Crest books, a division of The Salvation Army's National Publications department, was established in 1997 so contemporary Salvationist voices could be captured and bound in enduring form for future generations, to serve as witnesses to the continuing force and mission of the Army.

Stephen Banfield and Donna Leedom, *Say Something*

Judith L. Brown and Christine Poff, eds., *No Longer Missing: Compelling True Stories from The Salvation Army's Missing Persons Ministry*

Terry Camsey, *Slightly Off Center! Growth Principles to Thaw Frozen Paradigms*

Marlene Chase, *Pictures from the Word; Beside Still Waters: Great Prayers of the Bible for Today; Our God Comes: And Will Not Be Silent*

John Cheydleur and Ed Forster, eds., *Every Sober Day Is a Miracle*

Helen Clifton, *From Her Heart: Selections from the Preaching and Teaching of Helen Clifton*

Shaw Clifton, *Never the Same Again: Encouragement for New and Not–So–New Christians; Who Are These Salvationists? An Analysis for the 21st Century; Selected Writings, Vol. 1: 1974-1999 and Vol. 2: 2000-2010*

Christmas Through the Years: A War Cry Treasury

Stephen Court and Joe Noland, eds., *Tsunami of the Spirit*

Frank Duracher, *Smoky Mountain High*

Easter Through the Years: A War Cry Treasury

Ken Elliott, *The Girl Who Invaded America: The Odyssey Of Eliza Shirley*

Ed Forster, *101 Everyday Sayings From the Bible*

William W. Francis, *Celebrate the Feasts of the Lord: The Christian Heritage of the Sacred Jewish Festivals; The Stones Cry Out*

Henry Gariepy, *Israel L. Gaither: Man with a Mission; A Salvationist Treasury: 365 Devotional Meditations from the Classics to the Contemporary; Andy Miller: A Legend and a Legacy*

Henry Gariepy and Stephen Court, *Hallmarks of The Salvation Army*

Roger J. Green, *The Life & Ministry of William Booth* (with Abingdon Press, Nashville)

How I Met The Salvation Army

Carroll Ferguson Hunt, *If Two Shall Agree* (with Beacon Hill Press, Kansas City)

John C. Izzard, *Pen of Flame: The Life and Poetry of Catherine Baird*

David Laeger, *Shadow and Substance: The Tabernacle of the Human Heart*

John Larsson, *Inside a High Council; Saying Yes to Life*

Living Portraits Speaking Still: A Collection of Bible Studies

Herbert Luhn, *Holy Living: The Mindset of Jesus*

Philip Needham, *He Who Laughed First: Delighting in a Holy God,* (with Beacon Hill Press, Kansas City); *When God Becomes Small*

R.G. Moyles, *I Knew William Booth; Come Join Our Army; William Booth in America: Six Visits 1886 - 1907; Farewell to the Founder*

Joe Noland, *A Little Greatness*

Quotes of the Past & Present

Lyell M. Rader, *Romance & Dynamite: Essays on Science & the Nature of Faith*

R. David Rightmire, *Sanctified Sanity: The Life and Teaching of Samuel Logan Brengle*

Allen Satterlee, *Turning Points: How The Salvation Army Found a Different Path; Determined to Conquer: The History of The Salvation Army Caribbean Territory; In the Balance: Christ Weighs the Hearts of 7 Churches*

Harry Williams, *An Army Needs An Ambulance Corps: A History of The Salvation Army's Medical Services*

A. Kenneth Wilson, *Fractured Parables: And Other Tales to Lighten the Heart and Quicken the Spirit; The First Dysfunctional Family: A Modern Guide to the Book of Genesis, It Seemed Like a Good Idea at the Time: Some of the Best and Worst Decisions in the Bible*

A Word in Season: A Collection of Short Stories

Check Yee, *Good Morning China*

Chick Yuill, *Leadership on the Axis of Change*